(1)

Mike Weiford's parenting book is a gift! As a parent educator and neuroscience-informed treatment provider, I am constantly on the search for both accurate and accessible work for my clients. This book meets the mark for both in spades! Weiford lays out holistic understanding of child development in understandable, bite-sized pieces. He sprinkles insights for addressing various parenting issues throughout with clarity and an invitation to play along by providing questions to ponder —and actually answer —along the way. He then goes on to introduce new ways of thinking about discipline, encouraging the reader to think of parenting in a positive and visionary yet realistic manner. His inclusion of heartfelt experience alongside conventional wisdom makes new perspectives instantly relatable and understandable. The reader feels cared for and guided rather than forced heavy handedly into a particular line of thought. All in all a deep read made stress-free by the very personal nature of the writing. A must-read for anyone who interacts in a meaningful way with children!

—Hannah Smith, MA, LMHC, CGP

(2)

I have known Mike over twenty years and have seen the principles in these carefully worded pages work and provide tools of hope for parents and caregivers. You will be encouraged with strategies that provide a loving, effective system of discipline. There is HOPE for your situation.

—Gregory L. Jantz, PhD, C.E.D.S. Founder,
The Center * A Place of HOPE

(3)

Finally, a clear and down-to-earth roadmap for parents who seek a godly route through both the inevitable and avoidable minefields life puts in our paths! Mike has certainly woven his vast experience through this profoundly valuable book. I highly recommend it for parents and caregivers of any aged child as a best-practice guidebook.

—Darci Jones, LMHC

NAVIGATING
the
MINEFIELD

To Marianne —
Thanks for your
friendship at NCWA —

Blessings,

Mike Weaver

NAVIGATING
the
MINEFIELD

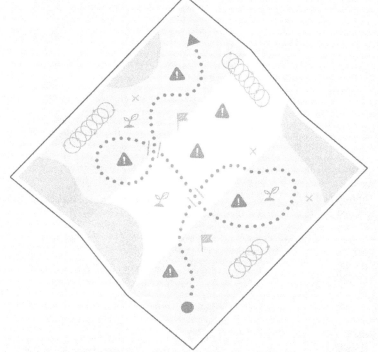

A Map for Effective Parenting
WITH CHILD DEVELOPMENT UPDATES

MIKE WEIFORD

REDEMPTION
PRESS

Published by Redemption Press, PO Box 427, Enumclaw, WA 98022.
Toll-Free (844) 2REDEEM (273-3336)

Redemption Press is honored to present this title in partnership with the author. The views expressed or implied in this work are those of the author. Redemption Press provides our imprint seal representing design excellence, creative content, and high-quality production.

The author has tried to recreate events, locales, and conversations from memories of them. In order to maintain their anonymity, in some instances the names of individuals, some identifying characteristics, and some details may have been changed, such as physical properties, occupations, and places of residence.

ISBN 13: 978-1-64645-455-6 (Paperback)
978-1-64645-456-3 (ePub)
978-1-64645-457-0 (Mobi)

Library of Congress Catalog Card Number: 2021914147

To all children on the journey toward adulthood—and to the parents and caregivers who help and guide them along the way. May you live the life you were given to live.

Contents

Acknowledgments

I want to thank my wife, Judy, for her love and support that empowers me to help others and for her labor of love in transcribing the first draft of this manuscript from my handwritten notes. Our son, Chris, also gifted countless hours of graphic design work, which transformed the manuscript into a workable and presentable format. He also designed the folded map on the front cover and the icon illustrations at the beginning of each chapter. Thank you.

Erin Brown, a freelance editor, provided invaluable assistance on this journey toward publication by polishing the content. Darci Jones offered encouragement when life presented barriers to the writing process, and she gave permission to incorporate her material related to parent-infant bonding.

Shout-out of thanks to our daughter, Valerie, and to Dr. Glen Van Andel, PhD, for their constructive input on the manuscript. And to all my supportive friends and colleagues who graciously reviewed portions of *Navigating the Minefield* and offered refining feedback—thank you.

Special thanks go to Dr. Gregory Jantz, PhD, founder of The Center • A Place of HOPE, for being one of the early voices encouraging me in this writing journey. Dr. Jantz and The Center provided an environment for life-changing teamwork and gave me permission to incorporate the positive system of discipline presented in chapter 8 of *Navigating the Minefield*. It has been a privilege and blessing to be a member of The Center's whole-person clinical care team for the past thirty-two years. More healing teamwork ahead.

To the Redemption Press team who helped bring this project to print and the light of day: Athena, Karen, Tammy, Dori, Jen, Jon, and company—many thanks.

Crossing the Minefields

A *New York Times* article confirms that in 2016 there were sixty-four countries where un-cleared landmines were known to exist.[1] The article goes on to document that in 2015, more than one-third of the total 6,461 civilians who were killed or wounded by landmines were children. These are statistics on physical landmines.

But throughout human history, families in every generation have also faced "landmines"—various threats, barriers, and challenges on the road to successfully bringing their children from birth to adulthood. These landmines can include anything that directly harms a child or blocks the child's healthy growth and development. Disease, poverty, lack of education, abuse, neglect, and exposure to addictions are a few examples of such landmines. The metaphor of a minefield illustrates the seriousness of the risks to our children's physical and emotional health and security.

Other landmines threaten children and their families, such as a child's exposure to environmental toxins like lead-based paint, mold, and contaminated water. Landmines can also include a child's vulnerability to bullying in the neighborhood or at school or from online cyber-bullying, gangs, sexual predators, exposure to addictions, emotional abuse, reactive anger, or exposure to violence—like the suicide of a family member or violence between members of the child's household.

Here in the United States of America, the events of September 11, 2001, tragically ushered in a new era of violence and uncertainty. The great recession that started in 2008 also triggered shockwaves of home foreclosures and unemployment that were felt for many years. Though the economy has been rebuilding, the advent of a tariff war and growing economic uncertainty makes people question when the next major downturn might hit. Threats of terrorism and economic hardship can also be counted among the examples of landmines.

By March 2020 the novel coronavirus and the associated COVID-19 disease had become a skyrocketing global pandemic. It is still unclear how long it will take for the virus to become contained and managed. With children home from school and forced into concentrated interaction with family at home to prevent the spread of the virus, stress levels for parents and children have been on the rise.

For many, the world has become an unpredictable and insecure place. The impact of these threats on the public welfare of families is profound. Parents often face significant challenges when providing for their children's basic needs of housing, education, food, access to quality healthcare, and clean water. In reality, we all have been directly or indirectly impacted by various landmines from living in this world. The imagery of dangerous landmines helps to underscore that all of us in this democratic society need to take threats to our children's well-being seriously. Though some children sadly do not survive to see adulthood, many individuals impacted by trauma recover with the benefit of treatment and loving support. While we are not able to control events around us, we have hope knowing some landmines are preventable.

Perhaps your personal story involves wounds received from the actions of others, and you now experience anxiety about providing care for a child or adolescent. Maybe you are a single parent and feeling alone in your parenting journey. Or you might be a grandparent stepping up to provide a home for your grandchild or a couple considering starting a family but anxious about the prospect of raising a child in today's world. Perhaps you are a parent living with regrets regarding past parenting mistakes—in need of forgiveness—while learning how to prevent repeating those mistakes in your current parenting. More than ever, parents need help traversing this "minefield." They need hope-giving resources and encouragement to equip them. The intent of *Navigating the Minefield* is to be such a resource.

At the heart of this project is the celebration of the precious children in our lives. You will discover passionate encouragement in these pages as you navigate the dangers on the road to bringing your children to adulthood. By better understanding your child's developmental needs, you will be better equipped to embrace one of life's greatest joys.

It is also my desire to include helpful information related to child development. Because parenting that is sensitive to a child's developmental needs is more effective parenting, part 2 of the book contains summaries of the physical, emotional, and cognitive development for each stage of childhood and adolescence.

This project flows from forty years of clinical work, including a significant focus on children, adolescents, parents, and families, written in stages over a twenty-two-year period. A variety of encouraging voices challenged me to write an inspiring parenting book. Some projects require a full measure of time and seasoning before they are complete. This is one such project.

One of the driving passions behind writing this book was introducing and promoting the positive system of discipline, presented in part 4. With this system of discipline, a parent will be reasonably equipped to help develop and activate a child's conscience. My experience shows that using this system of discipline can also help demonstrate what forgiveness in a family looks like.

What You Will Learn
- What "landmines" are and how they may pose a risk to the health, safety, and well-being of children in your care
- Child development basics to inform your understanding of children's developmental needs and help you support their healthy growth

- How to promote a strong emotional bond with your infant
- Positive discipline options that will empower you to be confident in your parental role, resulting in a reduced risk of abuse and neglect for future generations
- How to develop a positive vision for a child's future, including identifying outcome goals for nurturing healthy character traits
- Support, encouragement, and grace for caregivers who have regrets related to past parenting mistakes
- Strategies for being more effective in raising the children in your care

Currently, I work as a senior clinician as part of a multidisciplinary, whole-person team in The Center's intensive program. This includes significant work with parents who struggle with their health and self-care. Often, the individuals for whom I provide care are parents who need reminders of God's grace. The parenting job description and parental role performance evaluation found in part 5 contains much of the material related to helping restore a person's sense of self-esteem and self-compassion.

A key source of inspiration for the book you hold in your hand is the gift that my wife, Judy, and I have been given in raising our precious children—our two sons, Chris and Nathan, and our daughter, Valerie. In my experience, trust in a loving, powerful, and responsive God has allowed Judy and me to live and raise our family with enough peace and security as not to let fear and worry paralyze us.

I also acknowledge and honor the fact that most experts on having children (midwives, moms, and medical professionals) and lovingly nurturing and raising children (moms, nannies, grandmothers, sisters, aunts and other extended family members, childcare workers, medical professionals, etc.) are women. Certainly, male researchers and theorists are well-represented in the study and care of children. I want to honor the women in our world who have often led the way in demonstrating compassionate care for children. The influence of nurturing and compassionate women has helped to socialize the human community. More fathers are becoming actively involved in nurturing and raising their children, including infants. As one of these nurturing and involved dads, I know how it feels to carry the weight of responsibility for a helpless newborn, totally dependent upon my wife and me for life, care, and survival.

An experience my wife and I had as first-time parents while living in Western Michigan illustrates this powerfully. Our firstborn, back when we called him Christopher, was approximately three months old. Suddenly, in the middle of a November night, my wife and I were awakened by the horrifying sound of our precious newborn gasping for air and barking like a seal. We quickly called our pediatrician, who told us to bring Christopher to the emergency room of our local hospital and to roll down the windows so the cool night air could help him breathe. By the time we arrived at the hospital, our son was breathing normally and no longer barking. The medical team diagnosed croup, administered respiratory therapy treatment, and discharged our son to our care.

That experience with croup was one of our first initiations to parenthood. It humbled us with the new and overwhelming awareness of just how vulnerable our newborn babe was and how utterly dependent he was on us for his health and survival. Perhaps you can relate. Our first experience with croup was shocking, our first landmine as parents. The experience also reinforced the importance of quick access to knowledgeable medical care providers for our little one.

Years of clinical experience with those who have been hurt by various landmines has also given me perspective on how fragile life is. I know the importance of education and resources that help to reduce risks to our children and our children's children.

Minefield Hypothetical

Understanding the concept of "stewardship" in our parental role is key to better understanding our responsibility for the precious lives temporarily placed in our care to protect, nurture, and raise to adulthood. Stewardship, then, includes the "careful and responsible management of something entrusted to one's care" (*Merriam-Webster's*

Collegiate Dictionary, eleventh edition). The minefield hypothetical illustrates this. In our role as entrusted stewards, parents have the privilege and responsibility to nurture and protect the children in our care. The following imaginary story illustrates how we need God's help in our parenting task, which often shows up through a supportive community. The imagination can be used to help us emotionally connect, through story, with a value or principle.

You are visiting some of your dearest and closest friends who have moved with their young children to one of those sixty-four countries with unexploded landmines near their towns. One morning during your visit, you agree to watch your friends' two small children, with whom you have become attached, while the parents go to the town's market in the early morning hours. While your friends are still at the market, a military action suddenly breaks out, and your neighborhood is ordered to evacuate. The main road to the market district has been closed, and armed soldiers are barricading the way. Your mission is to deliver your friends' children to them at the market. While you hurriedly pack a backpack with food, water, clothing, and other supplies, you cry out to God for help in your distress, as the situation is beyond what you can handle on your own. Just then the elderly, kind, and wise neighbor from next door appears at your door, urging you to follow with the children. The neighbor knows the way through a section of the old minefield to get to the market district. The alternative of being separated from your dear friends is overwhelming. The only way now to get to the market district is to trust the kind neighbor who will lead you and the children through the old minefield. Because of the neighbor's wise guidance in navigating the minefield, you reunite with your dear friends.

When we accept the responsibility to care for the children of beloved friends in desperate circumstances, we become extremely focused on our mission and feel the weight of that duty on a whole new level. It can be sobering to parent our children with the perspective that children are not our personal property but gifts from God. And we have the sacred opportunity to care for them in the best way possible, as good parents and stewards—with God's help. The helpful neighbor in our story represents answered prayer and the many resources we can tap into to guide us on our parenting journey.

PART 1

Stages of Child Development (Birth through Preschool Age)

CHAPTER 1

Celebrating the Miracle of Life

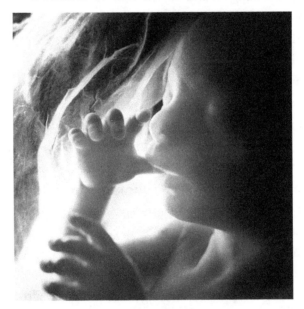

O LORD, you have searched me and you know me. . . . even the darkness will not be dark to you . . . For you created my inmost being; you knit me together in my mother's womb. . . . My frame was not hidden from you when I was made in the secret place.

Psalm 139:1, 12–13, 15 NIV

A picture *is* worth a thousand words, at the very least. Lennart Nilsson, the renowned medical and scientific photographer, published the above photo and many other in utero photos in *A Child Is Born*.[2] The cover includes the caption: "Dramatic Photographs of Life before Birth." Look closely at the spectacular photo again. It is the photo of a living four-and-one-half-month-old unborn child, just over seven inches long. The authors of *A Child Is Born* observe that at this stage "when the thumb comes close to the mouth, the head may turn, and lips and tongue begin their sucking motions."[3]

The infant's first home address: a mother's womb. The nutrient-rich environment of the uterus is the transitional housing of every child who is born. This is the awesome equalizer of the human race. The common denominator. Every child who has been born has emerged from such an inner room. Another amazing thought that we easily forget is that you and I started our life journey from the very same kind of secret room. We've come a long way, baby!

In this chapter, we will review a description of the growth and development of the human fetus during gestation. Barbara M. Newman and Philip R. Newman formed a husband-and-wife partnership in the research and teaching of human development over the life span. It is their text *Development Through Life: A Psychosocial Approach*, Revised Edition, from which I draw much of the material on child development. The Newman's foundation for their perspective on the psychological stages of life comes from the psychosocial theory of growth and development as presented by Erik H. Erickson, who organized his theory of human development around eight life stages. The Newmans expanded on Erickson's life stages by differentiating between early adolescence (approximately ages 11–16) and later adolescence (approximately ages 17–22). They also integrated research regarding the progressive growth and development of the human during gestation. Following is a brief overview of the nine months from conception to birth.[4]

First Trimester
- Divisions of the cell
- Attachment to the lining of the uterus begins (by the sixth day)
- Growth of the amniotic sac, which fills with clear watery fluid that serves as the fluid shock absorber for the embryo (by three weeks)

- Growth of the placenta, an organ designed for the exchange of nutrients from the mother's blood and release of waste material from the embryo (by three weeks)
- Emergence of body parts and differentiation of sex organs
- Movement
- Grasp reflex
- Babinski reflex (the sign of an emerging nervous system; stimulation of the sole of the foot results in a fanning of the toes by three months)
- Heartbeat
- Average size at three months: three inches, fourteen grams

Second Trimester

- Sucking and swallowing
- Preference for sweet taste (at four months)
- Skin ridges on fingers and toes
- Hair on scalp, eyebrows, back, arms, and legs
- Sensitivity to touch, taste, light
- Sucks thumb
- Average size at six months: ten inches, two pounds

Third Trimester

- Nervous system matures
- Coordination of stronger sucking response and swallowing
- Body temperature regulation
- More efficient digestion and excretion
- Degeneration of the placenta toward the end of the ninth month
- Baby boy brain testosterone wash, resulting in fewer connections between the right and left hemispheres (on average)
- Average size at nine months: twenty inches, seven to seven-and-a-half pounds—acknowledging a great deal of variability in the sizes of "full-term" infants

The implications from a study of human development during gestation are profound, causing us to reflect on such things as the amazing design of the human being while developing in the womb and the importance of the mother's health and nutrition to support the baby's healthy development. It is a myth that the developing unborn baby will always receive what it needs regardless of what the pregnant woman eats. Obtaining professional medical and nutritional support is essential for adequate prenatal care and nutrition during pregnancy.

Brain Science Update

In their coauthored book *Raising Boys by Design*, Dr. Gregory Jantz, PhD, and Michael Gurian present an eye-opening summary of research related to the differences between male and female brains. Jantz and Gurian provide an excellent discussion of how these distinctive design differences can help parents and educators better understand, honor, and respond to the learning differences between males and females. Following is a brief summary of some of the differences between boy's and girls' brains[5]:

- Boy's brains tend to use seven times more localized gray matter (on the left hemisphere) for processing activity.
- Girl's brains tend to use about ten times more white brain matter from all over the brain—which connects gray matter to emotion and verbal communication centers on both hemispheres for processing activity.
- Boys have up to twenty times as much testosterone (sex drive and aggression hormone).
- Girls have significantly more estrogen (female growth and reproductive hormone) and significantly more oxytocin (a bonding-relationship hormone).
- Boys process less of the bonding hormone (oxytocin) on average.
- Girls have a larger hippocampus (center for holding memory).
- Girls tend to use more words when communicating about an event, feeling, person, story, thing, or place.

- Male brains tend to shift to a boredom state (brain centers becoming less activated and major brain activity significantly shuts down) more often than female brains.

Gurian coined the term *bridge brains* to describe those individuals, both female and male, "whose neural functions seem more like, and actually scan more like, the other gender."[6] Researchers are finding a spectrum of male brains and a spectrum of female brains. Approximately four out of five male brains reflect the male brain profile, and four out of five female brains reflect the female brain profile. Gurian makes the point that exceptions help to prove a statistical rule. Approximately 20 percent of all male brains are bridge brains that may result in a boy with a bridge brain being more comfortable sitting calmly and able to use many words to process and express feelings, emotions, and detailed memories of past experiences.[7] Gurian's findings are important information for us as parents. Twenty percent of males are comfortable expressing themselves verbally in similar ways to females. The other 80 percent of males process and communicate emotions differently. It is helpful to know what type of male brain your son has.

CHAPTER 2

Infants (Birth–2 Years)

The term *child development* refers to science-based observations of children in modern industrialized societies and across cultures, socioeconomic backgrounds, and geography regarding how children develop physically, emotionally, and mentally from birth to early adulthood. For our purposes, we will discuss the sequential developmental tasks and the psychosocial "crisis," or tension, between the child's developmental abilities and needs versus the social expectations of the culture or community. I will summarize this developmental information for each stage of childhood development. This section will consider the life stage of infancy, which extends up to twenty-four months.

Following are the four developmental tasks associated with an infant's physical and emotional growth:

- **Develop a significant social attachment with the primary caregiver(s) who expresses "warmth and affection toward the child."**[8] From birth to three months old, the infant initiates behaviors of sucking, rooting (wanting to nurse), grasping, smiling, staring at caregiver's face and eyes, and cuddling to interact and gain closeness with the caregiver.[9]
- **Develop behaviors that connect cause and effect.** An example is discovering that if they let go of a spoon, it falls to the floor. Babies begin to connect that when they cry, a primary caregiver will come. Babies' use of different cries (you will come to learn

them) is their primary and natural way to get their needs met. The infant needs to learn through experience that someone will show up to help in response to a cry. This is experiential trust. When a child consistently experiences neglect—when they do not receive a response to cries due to feeling hungry, having a wet or soiled diaper, being too cold or hot, feeling lonely, or feeling threatened in some way—it is damaging. There is a positive return for responsive parents: studies have found that caregivers who responded promptly to infants' cries in the first six months had babies who cried less often in the second six months.[10]

- **Develop a sense that people and things (objects) have a permanent reality and do not pop in and out of existence based on whether they can be seen, touched, or heard.** Object permanence is developed in the average infant at approximately nine to ten months of age. The game of peekaboo is a fresh surprise every time for the infant who has not yet developed object permanence, as the person or thing that is hidden seems to no longer exist. They don't look for the hidden thing until they cognitively understand that the hidden thing is still there but that it is hiding. Once object permanence is developed, the child tends to keep searching for the hidden object in games like hide-and-seek— making for a new form of fun.

- **Develop primary motor function.** Jean Piaget, the French engineer-turned-child-development researcher and expert, constructed a theory of sensorimotor intelligence in infancy, which is regarded as foundational to understanding infant development. He observed that infants develop intelligence related to physical movement and interaction with their environment.[11] Following is a list of typical developmental milestones for physical movement from birth to age two[12]:

Coordination of sucking response, including adjusting to breast or bottle (see also: *The Womanly Art of Breastfeeding*)	1–2 weeks

Ability to hold head up	2 months
Ability to roll over	4 months
Ability to reach and grasp	5 months
Ability to sit up alone	7 months
Ability to crawl (Crawling helps develop strong back muscles, so do not attempt to rush a child to walk earlier than ready.)	10 months
Ability to stand alone	14 months
Ability to cruise along with furniture	14.5 months
Ability to walk alone	15 months
Ability to run alone	18 months
Ability to climb alone	2 years

The psychosocial "crisis" for the life stage of infancy is "Trust versus Mistrust." [13] As we have already introduced, over time, the infant will develop experiential trust that her caregivers will respond to and figure out which needs are screaming for attention. The opposite is also possible. Under severe and extended conditions, the infant can learn to mistrust the environment and lack confidence in caregivers to consistently meet needs and give comfort. Consistent mistrust over time may show itself in the form of symptoms of concern by the infant, such as "withdrawal from interaction and symptoms of depression and grief, which may include sobbing, lack of emotion, lethargy, and loss of appetite."[14]

The infant's behaviors will confirm that a significant social attachment with the caregiver(s). The infant will

- make efforts to maintain contact with the caregiver;
- show distress when the person of attachment is absent; and
- respond differently to people in the environment—they will be more relaxed and at ease with persons of attachment and more unsettled with people to whom there is not an attachment.[15]

Researcher M. E. Lamb made an interesting discovery in 1976 regarding fathers and their infants. He observed that infants were more playful and smiled and laughed when looking at their fathers. He also noted that infants were more focused on comfort-and stress-reducing interactions with their mothers.[16] Apart from households in which the father is the primary caregiver, I suggest this would generally be true today. Of course, many variables impact father-child interactions, including the father's personality and level of involvement. Fortunately, we are seeing a significant increase in many dads' positive involvement with their infants.

Parents' primary responsibility is to nurture their children's psychological health, whose helplessness at birth demands an extended period of dependence on us. The infant's relative lack of advanced behaviors driven by instinct, such as the newborn's inability to move on her own power, is balanced out by an enormous inborn capacity to learn. For this tremendous potential for learning to be actualized, infants must depend upon their parents and caregivers to maintain their health, provide interaction, and protect them from danger. Parents have the key role in promoting a strong emotional bond with their infants and nurturing their children's intellectual growth.

Parents encourage social attachment by responding consistently and promptly to their infants' needs. Parents accomplish this by actively holding and cuddling their infants and by looking at, smiling at, and talking to them. Parents who take an interest in their infants' well-being will expend large amounts of energy to get their infants to smile.[17] When an infant has formed a secure emotional attachment with a primary caregiver, the child is equipped to gradually venture out to explore her environment, thereby stimulating the cognitive growth of her brain and senses.[18]

Gazing into the eyes of your infant stimulates brain development and forms new neural pathways. Babies love looking at human faces and have an amazing capacity for face recognition.[19] Many wonderful developmental-friendly toys and gadgets are available today as supplements. However, it is key to remember that for a sighted infant—nothing is quite the same as gazing into the eyes of a live person.

Infants need to experience their parents as mature and consistent enough to communicate to them messages of acceptance and forgiveness even in those times when their parents "lose it." This is especially important when the child acts against the parent's directions and wishes, which can result in frustration and stress for the parent. The infant's developmental need is to be able to trust the parent enough to be counted on, especially through stressful times. The child that is sixteen months to two-and-a-half years old is especially sensitive to his parent's responses during times of conflict. If a parent were to withdraw from the infant, giving verbal or non-verbal messages of rejection like silent treatment or avoidance, the result could be highly detrimental to the child's ability to trust others. The risk particularly increases with repeated experiences over time. It is our job to be mature enough not to hold grudges against our children. We need to be predictable enough that our young children can trust that we will be there for them, providing loving care and acceptance after their behavior has stressed us out. We must be the mature parent, the adult. The foundation we give our children in being trustworthy to provide consistently adequate, nurturing care contributes to their ability to trust others throughout their lives.

If your tendency is to withdraw and zone out with alcohol or some other mood-altering substance when under stress, I encourage you to seek support in your area to have any potential substance-use problem evaluated and addressed before the pattern escalates. An increasing number of adults who have reached out for such support— including parents—are successfully discovering practical relief and healthy coping skills.

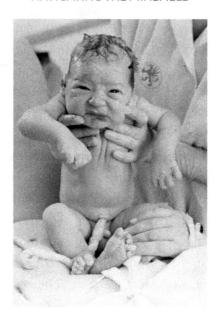

Revisiting Newborns

I love the above picture. It is a wet and sloppy reminder of reality. This is what a one-minute-old baby boy looks like after being squeezed out of the birth canal. You'd look like that, too, if you'd gone through what he just had!

Researchers at the Stanford Vision and Neurodevelopment Lab found that newborns less than an hour old tend to stare at face-like images more than any other pattern. They also discovered that newborns recognize their mothers' faces more quickly than they do adult female strangers.[20] Study the picture. The baby is wired to look for a reassuring face. Look at his eyes. He is intently looking at his mother's face.

Numerous child development researchers through the years have discovered that the average human newborn is capable of
- responding to movement, able to visually track a bright object, such as a bright red ball;[21]
- detecting changes in loudness and pitch (high or low) of sound;[22] and

- responding to specific phonetic sounds of speech, such as the contrast between vowel sounds.[23]

I had the privilege of working with Darci Jones when she worked at The Center for Counseling and Health Resources, now called The Center • A Place of HOPE, as a member of our clinical team. Her particular area of passion and specialty is parent-infant attachment and bonding, of which she writes:

> What many new parents may really need is a listening ear, validation that they are doing a good job, someone to help when they feel overwhelmed, a friend. Sleep deprivation and limited resources can exaggerate problems in an otherwise healthy relationship. The earlier a problem is noticed, the greater the chance of successful intervention.
>
> Severe attachment problems are atypical and may require frequent in-home psychotherapy and support services. It is important to remember that not all attachment problems are the result of abuse or neglect. For this reason, it is important to complete a developmental screening with a skilled provider prior to diagnosing specific attachment disorders. There may be medical, neurological, or sensory problems within the infant that mimic, cause, or predispose an infant to develop attachment difficulties. Specific screening tools are used to help determine the primary problem.
>
> When problems are identified early in an infant's life, the chance of leading a normal life increases greatly. Screening tools (when used by a trained professional) can also identify sensory problems that could interfere with attachment and can be treated by a sensory integration specialist.

She goes on to state that the parent's mental and physical health also affects the attachment relationship. Severe symptoms, such as postpartum depression, can develop suddenly. It can be difficult, she suggests, to tell the difference between depression, hormonal imbalance, or sleep deprivation.

Not all infants and parents with adjustment challenges need psychotherapy. Rather, they may need assistance in finding the type of services that would be helpful for their particular situation. When seeking these specialized services, it is helpful for parents to know that infant-parent dyadic attachment therapy is a specialty that requires an advanced clinical degree along with either certification or specialized training in infant mental health. Developmental screeners may have a bachelor's degree or above. She recommends a treatment team approach that includes input from all of the available providers to give support to the family. She acknowledges the University of Washington as one of several quality programs that has an excellent master's degree level certification program in infant-parent attachment assessment and therapy. Any quality program like this would also have referrals for qualified providers. Ms. Darci Jones has done an excellent job of summarizing an educational overview of baby-parent attachment with practical ideas in her handout, "Emotional Development of Infants and Toddlers." With her permission, I am including a significant excerpt from that document here:

> Another reason for babies to have emotional insecurity is when a parent is feeling overwhelmed by depression, unresolved grief or trauma, uncontrolled impulses, addictions, high stress or anger. Often, both baby and parent factors are influencing the infant's emotional development and attachment.
>
> And just like babies, parents need to feel safe, secure, and loved to feel confident and to be emotionally available for baby, to feel comfortable playing and interacting joyfully, to be able to really listen and hear what baby is feeling. Everyone wants to love and be loved. It is easiest for parents to feel loving when they feel loved.

It helps to have caring support from the other parent, friends, family, neighbors, etc. Someone to talk to, a shoulder to cry on, someone to laugh with. This helps you to reduce stress and feel more relaxed. When you feel relaxed, baby can feel relaxed, also. When you feel anxious, baby feels anxious too!

When you don't have family or friends to rely on and to lean on it is harder to find the support you need, and, it is harder to give and receive love. If you have experienced abuse or have other unresolved issues from your past or present, it will be harder to be consistently able to give love, to be able to understand baby's feelings, and, to confidently communicate with baby.

All relationships are based on communication of both feelings and thoughts. Babies can only communicate without words. They "talk" with their bodies, with gestures, facial expressions, noises, and cries. Learning to communicate with a baby takes lots of looking, watching, patience, and time. But time can be a rare commodity that slips by us when we aren't looking.

Slowing down your lifestyle to spend more fun times together now will pay off in the long run. Both you and baby will feel less stress when not hurried through life and will enjoy each other more. Making feeding and diapering fun sets the tone for later play. Babies and children communicate and learn about their emotions through interactive and make-believe play. They need lots of happy play with their parent(s) to grow up with healthy emotions.

Social competence in childhood is based on what baby experiences with you. Make it fun! Babies watch everything you say and do. They learn by imitating you, and, by responding to how safe and loved they feel when attempting to interact with you.

Unfortunately, many adults did not get to play as children and do not really know how. A playgroup is a great way to learn how. There are books and videos too. It can be fun to learn to play. Remember that play is the "work" of babies and children! Play is also very important to parents in relieving stress!

Parents need leisure time away from their babies too.

New brain research shows that our brains control our bodies, intelligence, and emotions. The parts that regulate emotions are very sensitive and ready for rapid growth at birth but only grow in healthy ways when the baby feels safe and secure. Anything that terrifies baby can cause the brain to overwork these emotional parts, flooding undeveloped areas with brain chemicals that can cause permanent damage (such as frequent flooding of the stress hormone, cortisol). Neglect, including ignoring or showing inappropriate emotions can cause underdevelopment of the baby's brain.

Overstimulation can cause anxiety and frustration. However, parents who are patient, sensitive to baby's needs and feelings, gentle and kind, who make time to talk, listen, play and hold their baby with love, have babies who grow up to be happier, healthier children. As adults, they are also better adjusted with higher self-esteem and confidence.

Help is available. Therapy can help you recover from an unpleasant or traumatic childhood so that it doesn't interfere with your relationship with your baby. And other services can help parents feel confident in caring for their babies. Developmental therapies are sometimes needed. If you have questions or concerns about your baby's development, please ask for help. Contact your local Family Resource Center.

The following list is from Jones's Infant Emotional Development Checklist (Birth to 24 Months). These are experiences and behaviors to nurture in the baby-tot-parent interaction:

- Stops crying easily when I comfort and hold him or her
- Nearly always snuggles and molds to my body when I hold him or her
- Does not stiffen or turn away from me when I pick him or her up
- Looks at me in the eye and we look at each other together
- Gazes/stares at my face and often watches my mouth when I talk
- Likes to play games like peekaboo and read stories; likes to play pretend with me
- Is alert and curious when awake and tries to get my attention (likes to go outside)
- Moods and needs are easy to figure out, and I can tell when my child is tired or sick
- Can comfort self when upset by sucking fingers, rocking, holding toy or blankie
- Turns toward my face when I talk; attempts to talk back
- Tells me know how much and when to snuggle

Parents who complete the checklist are invited to rate the frequency of the items on this list. I include them here as practical examples of attachment behaviors to help you increase the degree of awareness regarding healthy attachment behaviors in your infant-parent interaction.

We've all heard the expression, "It takes a village to raise a child." This saying pictures a community of caring adults who share the responsibility of parenting the children. However, to ensure the healthy development of a young child in most industrialized societies, the primary caregivers must attach and track with the infant.

If you're a new mom, you probably already know of the wide range of maternal intuition among women. Some women possess a high degree of motherly nurturing from a young age. Some women who did not have consistent motherly nurturing modeled for them—or motherly nurturing doesn't come naturally for them—might have to work harder to develop and cultivate mother-to-infant attachment skills.

Many fathers, especially in recent decades, are learning the skills and behaviors of bonding and attachment with their children. If dads can learn these vital child-rearing skills, then I want to encourage any mom who may be saying to herself, "I don't feel like I have a strong maternal drive; I'm scared to death of this parenting job because I don't know if I will make a good mom." If you desire for your child to thrive and be healthy, you already are a caring parent. With support from healthy mentors in your life and from supportive resources, you will be able to learn and develop the skills to be a capable parent.

"Good enough" parenting is a concept that can prevent unrealistic pressure and expectations to be a "perfect" parent and can prevent the guilt that results when perfection is elusive. I am not talking about settling for minimal effort. "Good enough" parenting demonstrates enough effectiveness to nurture and guide the child from childhood to adulthood. There is no perfect parent. *When*—not *if*—we make mistakes, we do well to learn from them and receive forgiveness.

CHAPTER 3

Toddlerhood and Preschool (2–4 Years)

If you have children in this age range, you know how busy they are. Walking, running, climbing, talking, playing—they are always on the go. Toddlers are also beginning to explore what they can do by themselves, develop language to communicate more effectively, and apply their impulse-control brakes.

The psychosocial crisis that describes the tension between this inborn drive of "No! I do myself," their feelings of insecurity, and their parent's expectations and exasperation is "Autonomy versus Shame and Doubt."[24] Toddlers work to gain confidence in an effort to control their world. The following are developmental tasks of toddlerhood:

- Self-control
- Language development
- Fantasy and play
- Elaboration of locomotion (getting around)

Self-Control

Toddlers, particularly by age three, are developing their ability to control their bodies and behavior. They are also developing a sense of their ability to influence and control their immediate environment. It is a normal part of toddlers' development to experience intense emotions that result in temper tantrums when a need is not immediately gratified. As a toddler begins to develop a basic understanding of the concept of time, she learns that she can get a need met after a delay.[25]

Language Development

Researchers suggest that, on average, the basics of a child's primary language are learned from eighteen months to three years of age. Children with the physical capacity for speech learn to talk in their own time. A child can be verbal early. I have also seen situations where a child was delayed in talking for himself, while his older siblings were very verbal. He perhaps didn't feel there was anything that needed to be added. Please consult with your child's pediatrician if you are concerned about any significant delays or challenges in your child's verbal communication development.

A child in this age range needs to use problem-solving skills to decode rules of grammar for the language spoken in the home. Language perception starts with the child's ability to tell the difference between sounds and sound combinations before understanding the meaning of the sounds.[26] The Newmans give an excellent summary of the connection between an accepting environment and a child's healthy emotional development when they write: "For the sake of the child's emerging self-concept, angry feelings must be allowed some form of legitimate expression. It is in the process of expressing angry feelings that children learn to control themselves and to channel these feelings into constructive rather than destructive activity. The development of autonomy requires an environment that accepts the total child, including authentic feelings of anger."[27] Toddlers have a valid need to verbalize feelings of anger in a manner that is accepted by the caregivers. It is an important step to shift from "acting out" the emotion with the body—for example, by smashing a toy on the floor while screaming—to using words to express the emotion.

Having an acceptable outlet for the child to express anger is one way the parent can support this shift without invalidating the child's emotion. Teach your child how to express his or her emotions appropriately. For example, say to your child, "Use your words. You can say: 'I'm mad!' Can you say that?" This gives the young child an acceptable avenue for expressing anger, which will help the child calm herself more quickly. This method of communicating intense emotion will also be helpful in the later stages of childhood.

When your child uses their words to express anger, it is an ideal time to apply positive reinforcement to encourage the desired behavior. For example, you can reply in an encouraging tone of voice: "Good job! Thanks for using your words. I'm really proud of you." Include positive physical touch, such as lightly resting your hand on their shoulder. Expecting a full hug may be premature when your little one is still angry. Teach your children new behaviors while reinforcing them with a dose of your supportive attention.

Verbal Instruction

Because toddlers and early preschoolers are not able to fully process and understand verbal instructions, it is important to give yourself—or your child's designated caregiver—permission to bring the child to where you want him or her to perform a certain task. The child may get distracted and truly forget verbal instruction. This is particularly true of complex tasks such as going to another room *and* brushing his or her teeth. By making time to go with your child and turn it into a fun activity, you keep the routine positive and prevent unnecessary stress and frustration for both parent and child.

Fantasy and Play

Play truly is the child's work and therapy for processing real life. Jean Piaget made observations regarding children's learning and cognitive (thinking) development. He observed that between the ages of two and six years of age, children develop five forms of representation:

1. Imitation (when the model being imitated is not present)
2. Mental images/pictures of ideas

3. Symbolic drawing
4. Symbolic play
5. Language [28]

Children are free to express what they have seen or experienced in the past by imitating what they saw, drawing it, or playing it out in fantasy. A child uses a private world of imagination to express and self-soothe when feeling distressed.

The most complex form of symbolic play involves the creation of an imaginary friend.[29] The most popular authors of children's books understand the child's world of imagination, fantasy, and pretend. The imaginary friend may be an animal, a person—such as another child—or some other character, complete with its own personality traits. An imaginary friend can serve several different functions. If your child creates an imaginary friend and discloses it to you, you have a wonderful opportunity to enter into your toddler's world by asking her about her friend. Remember, it can be the child's creative way of coping with a lack of other children to play with or as a psychological way to cope with stress, so "play along" rather than accuse the child of lying and storytelling. (Remember, good storytellers can earn big money in the adult world.) It is healthy for parents to develop some degree of comfort with imaginative play and to look for opportunities to engage the child on his level. Engaging in imaginative play will strengthen the emotional bond between your children and you and support their cognitive development—all while having fun.

Young toddlers and preschoolers often do their own thing when playing. Parallel play refers to individual play when more than one child is present, with each one doing their own thing. Other children can be present, but it is the older toddler/preschooler who is able to participate in playing together with other children. It is ideal for there to be enough toys in the play area for each child to have one. Being able to share a toy without a tantrum is an advanced skill. Understanding this helps caregivers prevent unnecessary scolding for "not sharing."

Elaboration of Locomotion

The fourth developmental task for toddlers is the refining of movement and how they get around. The tricycle and other toys with pedals that are safe give the toddler increased freedom of movement and are fun and versatile.[30] Additionally, many two-to-four-year-olds are introduced to skiing, skating, sledding, and dancing. Swimming has been introduced to some little ones in infancy, hence the term *water babies*.

Successful toilet training enhances a child's mobility and supports a measure of independence. The average child's sphincter muscles, which control the ability to hold on to and release feces, do not fully mature and function until eighteen months to two years of age.[31] Three elements are required for a child to master toilet training without frustration or anxiety:

1. The child's ability to control the sphincter muscles
2. The child's ability to communicate an understood signal to the caregiver when it is "time to go"
3. The child's ability to be aware of and respond to the bodily cues that elimination is imminent

Some children biologically can control elimination but can't be bothered to pull away from something they are enjoying to go to the bathroom. The Newmans summarize: "If parents wait to begin toilet training until the toddler shows signs of readiness in all areas, then the children are likely to see the task of toilet training as a source of pride and accomplishment rather than a struggle of wills."[32]

Toddlers possess a high energy drive to master a wide variety of activities, and they often develop rituals associated with tasks. They benefit from support in negotiating their way of doing things to mesh with parents' expectations. The motto: "I do it myself" or "I can do it myself" comes through behavior as well as language.

For the especially strong-willed child, remember to avoid a battle of wills by focusing on what the "point" or essential need is. Author and learning specialist Cynthia Ulrich Tobias, in her excellent parenting resource *You Can't Make Me (But I Can Be Persuaded): Strategies for Bringing Out the Best in Your Strong-Willed Child,* encourages parents to give their children options when assigning them a task. She urges parents not to get pulled into a losing battle of wills. Children benefit from consistent structure and routines. For example, attaching bath time and bedtime routines with snuggle reading times becomes meaningful bonding parts of the day for both the parent and the child.

PART 2

Stages of Development through Adolescence

CHAPTER 4

Early School Age (5–7 Years)

The educational level for children in this stage is generally from kindergarten through the second grade. Children in this age group can be especially fun to work with. Ask any passionate elementary school teacher, and they will tell you that the vast majority of these children are compliant, thrive on structure, want to please, and are eager to learn. Certainly, a child's level of adequate rest, nutrition, and absence of trauma in their lives significantly influences their behavior in the classroom.

For many, youth athletics are introduced at this age, like baseball. If you have seen a game of T-ball or remember playing it as a child, you know how entertaining it can be. Soccer, gymnastics, swimming, and martial arts are other good physical activities for this age.

A significant degree of socialization occurs in the early school-age development stage, in which the child begins to develop a greater degree of impulse control.

The psychosocial crisis, or tension, for early school-age children is "Initiative [child's exploring the world] versus Guilt."[33] The psychosocial developmental tasks of early school age include the following:

- Sex-role identification
- Early moral development

- Concrete operations
- Group play

Sex-Role Identification

Sex-role identification and gender identification are complex. A child's biology of chromosomes and genetic DNA coding is the foundation of a child's sex. Researchers have confirmed the presence of both estrogen (female hormone) and testosterone (male hormone) in both males and females.[34] Biology, then, contributes variables that impact how children develop their sense of maleness or femaleness.

Role Models

Social/cultural expectations, interpersonal relationships, and identification with primary caregivers also significantly influence the sex-role identification process. It is a natural process for little boys to want to be like their daddies. They often want to dress and shave like their dads. If a son does not see qualities in his father he wants to mimic, he may look elsewhere for role models. He needs to have enough positive attachment to his dad or another adult male figure to develop a sense of "we are more alike than we are different."

However, the fear factor complicates attachment.[35] For example, if a son feels significantly threatened by his father's anger and develops a persisting fear of him, the child may be at risk of two extremes in development. He may (a) not see enough similarities between himself and his father to promote positive sex-role identification, or (b) mimic the father's aggressive behavior as a way to gain his father's acceptance and protection. In the second scenario, the son is at risk for growing up to be a dominating bully like his father, driven by the psychological need to survive and obtain the love and acceptance of the powerful parent figure. But not all sons of a bully father go on to become bullies themselves. The issue has certainly garnered traction in contemporary literature, with several resources on the topic of the "father wound." (Christian author H. Norman Wright, a licensed marriage, family, and child therapist and certified trauma specialist, wrote *Healing for the Father Wound.*)

The same can be said of young girls who tend to identify with and mimic the mother figure in their lives. This is particularly true when the mother is predictable enough to meet the child's needs, resulting in trust. Girls also tend to look for acceptance from the father figures in their lives and may develop "daddy issues" in the absence of healthy love and unconditional acceptance.

These "Father wounds" or "mother wounds" resulting from parental absence, rejection, or neglect often follow the young person into their adult years. Healthy parenting patterns established early on can prevent lasting emotional wounds and expensive therapy bills later in life.

People have a built-in need for role models and heroes. Role models are found in every area of life: sports, science, music, human rights advocacy, faith, etc. Like it or not, athletes who excel and receive media coverage are role models, particularly for many youths. Sports celebrity brings a responsibility to be intentional regarding the powerful influence over the impressionable minds of young people—on and off the court or field. People tend to identify with people they want to be like. Developmentally, this need for role models is an important part of the early school-age years and continues to be a factor in development through adolescence and into adulthood.

Becoming more aware of child development needs and risk factors can be a powerful motivation for promoting education, prevention, and recovery for ourselves as parents and our communities.

Transgender Identity Issues

Any discussion of sex-role identification and gender identification does well to include acknowledgment of transgender identity issues. A transgender individual is a person who internally identifies with the opposite sex of their biological sex at birth—the individual consistently feels and perceives their internal sense of being male or female does not match their external sex assignment. Transgender individuals have increasingly come into the public eye, particularly related to high-profile sports figures. In 1975, professional tennis player Renée Richards underwent male to female sex reassignment surgery. She was denied entry into the 1976 US Open and took the decision to court. In 1977, the New York Supreme Court ruled in this historic case in favor of her right to compete in the Women's US Open. More recently, former champion of the US Men's 1976 Olympic decathlon Bruce Jenner came out publicly as being a transgender person and underwent hormone treatments as Caitlyn.

Transgender Brain

The end of chapter 1 introduced brain science information that included Michael Gurian's concept of the bridge brain. In his 2018 release *The Minds of Girls,* Gurian spends some time discussing the updated research that transgender individuals appear to have what he calls an "extreme bridge brain." An extreme brain bridge is a modified brain that bridges the sexes and the gender-identity continuum. Researchers estimate that transgender individuals comprise 0.3 to 0.7 percent of people worldwide who are born in a cross-sex body. Researchers used MRIs to observe brain responses to androstadienone, a steroid with pheromone-like properties that causes a different smell response in the hypothalamus of females and males. Trans adolescents responded to an odor as peers of their internally identified sex consistent with a transgender brain. Researchers noted that sex differences in how brains respond physiologically to odors cannot be influenced by one's training or environment.[36] Refer to *The Minds of Girls* by Michael Gurian for further information on the specifics of the brain research as it relates to sex and gender identification.

Early Moral Development

Several theories exist regarding moral development, the process by which a human being encounters external limits that govern behavior and then develops a sense of what is right and wrong (conscience) and the ability to empathize with the feelings (including pain) of another person. Cognitive theorist Lawrence Kohlberg proposed four stages of moral development:

1. Rewards and punishment
2. Following rules and opinions of influential authority figures
3. Internalizing the Golden Rule
4. Determining the greater good

Notably, a person does not automatically progress to the higher and more advanced stages simply based on age. Multiple external and internal factors shape an individual's ethical conduct, including individualized personality traits.

Let's examine these four stages more closely.

Stage 1: Rewards and punishment

Rewards and punishment (positive reinforcement and negative consequences) determine the person's behavior, which is shaped by the severity and consistency of the consequences. Kohlberg describes this stage as "pre-conventional thought." Young children operate from Stage 1, making behavior choices based upon external limits their caregivers place upon them. Behavioral reinforcement programs incorporating gold stars and reward prizes are practical examples of this. The child learns the positive reward is enough to motivate compliance with the behavioral goal. Rewards might include special one-on-one time with a parent or financial rewards that can be saved toward a special purchase or activity. It is wise to help children internalize a sense of right and wrong that is not dependent on what they get out of it or not getting caught.

The reality is rewards and punishment drive a significant portion of many adults' morality. This can include the individual who is motivated by the rewards of acceptance by a peer group that is using substances to excess. The need for acceptance by a peer group can outweigh the risks of health problems, job loss, or legal consequences. It can include the individual who consistently drives at excessive rates of speed and only slows down to the posted speed limit when there is a visible presence of law enforcement and the threat of an expensive speeding ticket fine and possible increase in insurance premiums. Conversely, it would be the person who drives within the speed limit to save money with low insurance premiums. Stage 1 morality can include the individual who only complies with tax laws when there is some evidence of a possible financial or legal consequence. Some adults operate by the distorted belief that if they have more money than others—the illusion of excessive wealth—then the law does not apply to them. They have a distorted perception of being immune from negative consequences, such as in the case of crooked financial institutions that believe they are "too big to fail." They all are operating from the developmentally stunted Stage 1 morality.

Stage 2: Following the rules and opinions of influential authority figures

An individual's behavioral choices are profoundly influenced by the opinions and beliefs of those in authority to children: parental figure; older sibling; teacher; pastor, priest, or rabbi; coach; etc. During the early school age, we can anticipate the child beginning to internalize the values of influential authority figures. This is demonstrated when the five-to seven-year-old child concludes that it is wrong to copy answers off of another student's work because the teacher has enforced this rule in the classroom. The teacher is simultaneously instilling the values of honesty and integrity in the students. Kohlberg describes this stage as "conventional thought."

Stage 3: Internalizing the Golden Rule

Stage 3 is evidenced when the individual makes judgments based upon principles of law, reciprocity (how their behavior affects other people), empathy, and human values. Principles of freedom and individual rights are a common focus. Regardless of age, when a person begins to internalize the Golden Rule (Do to others as you would have them do to you), that person is operating to a significant degree at Stage 3 of moral development.

Stage 4: Determining the greater good

Stage 4 is the most developed state of morality, which requires that a person weigh the benefit of more people than oneself. To operate from this perspective, the individual takes existing laws into account as well as internalized values. For example, compassion in the context of the greater good can conclude such values as it is better to solve family disputes with negotiation and not violence, exploitation of women is wrong (no matter how much money you have), consistent use of ethical business practices even when no one is auditing or checking up on you, and a willingness to sacrifice personal comfort to benefit others. Kohlberg refers to this higher stage of moral reasoning as "post-conventional thought." Individuals in high school and college are generally thought to be capable of the transition to the post-conventional stage of moral development.[37]

Most children in the five- to seven-year-old age range are likely to operate from Stage 1 and Stage 2 morality. Some children at this age with an active conscience may begin to try on Stage 3 morality: treating others the way they would like to be treated.

We know from life experience that just because a person attains a certain age does not guarantee moral development advancement. The system of discipline described in chapter 8 helps activate a child's conscience, promoting healthy moral development.

Concrete Operations

Jean Piaget, the same child development researcher and expert introduced when discussing infants in chapter 2, observed that early school-age children are capable of more complex thought processes. He refers to this intellectual development stage as concrete operational thought.[38] The newfound cognitive ability allows children to use principles of logic as they perceive, explore, and organize objects in the world around them. This level of intellectual functioning continues until approximately age twelve.

A word of caution for parents, teachers, coaches, and other adults working with young children: Keep expectations grounded in a realistic understanding of a child's age and emotional development. A young child may demonstrate advanced intellectual aptitude. Yet when a parent or other overly enthusiastic adult pushes the child to master skills they are not ready for or interested in, the outcome can be destructive. For example, pressuring a young child (age three) to write his numbers perfectly may result in him becoming frustrated and resentful. Unresolved resentment may undermine the relationship between the child and the well-intentioned parent.

Another word of warning is worthy of attention. Do not put unrealistic expectations on a child whose physical size is larger than typical for that age. Youth athletics is a setting where this issue can come into play. Consider the scenario of the five-year-old boy who is taller and bigger than his classmates. If the five-year-old is the same size as, say, a second-grader, it can be easy to think of him as being as capable as a seven- or eight-year-old in speed, hand-eye coordination, and cognitive processing. But having unrealistic expectations for performance can result in frustration for the child and the adult. A healthy example of reality check self-talk for the adult is: "That's right; he is only five."

Group Play

Children in this developmental stage use vivid imagination and fantasy in play and are also drawn to group games. These group games are different from team sports. Group games are competitions that result in an individual winner and can be played over and over again, giving opportunities for several children to have peer cooperation and interaction as well as a turn at being the "winner." Group games have basic, consistent rules and do not require the assistance of an adult.[39] While the names of group games may change over the decades, the classics include games like hide-and-seek, duck, duck, goose, red rover, and freeze tag. Our family loved playing the nighttime variation of flashlight tag with our three children and the neighborhood kids. The swing set with monkey bars in our backyard—which our children's maternal grandfather made—was "base." A person was "safe" if they touched the base before the person who was "it" could shine the flashlight on them and call out their name. Just thinking about some of those exciting and well-attended rounds of flashlight tag still brings me a feeling of joy and a smile to my face. And while that handmade swing set is no longer in our backyard, the fond memories of those evening neighborhood games will always stay with us. All we need to do is say: "Remember when we used to play flashlight tag?" and it all comes back.

It is the adults' responsibility to ensure children's play environment is safe. There will be times children will benefit from the freedom to experience the fun of group games without adult involvement. However, it is healthy for us parents to increase our comfort with play. We are healthier for it, physically and emotionally. When we embrace and participate in play, we model having fun to our children. It not only creates healthy alternatives to screen time, but the ability to play will serve children well for the rest of their lives.

As mentioned earlier in this chapter, the psychosocial "crisis" for the early school-age child is "Initiative versus Guilt." Erik Erikson uses the word "initiative" to describe the child's active initiation of investigation and exploration of their external environment. The child draws on the sense of confidence and autonomy nurtured in toddlerhood to successfully develop the ability to learn cause and effect and exert more self-control to avoid scolding and embarrassment by parents and teachers. This newfound skill is grounded in self-confidence, internalizing a code for behavior and the ability to reward himself for acceptable behavior.[40]

The "guilt" side of the continuum becomes pronounced when a child lacks the independence and courage to explore the world. The child may develop an overdependence on parents or other adults to prevent the uncomfortable experience of being scolded for socially inappropriate behavioral mistakes. This reinforces the benefits of a positive system of discipline that is grace-based and not shame-based. Chapter 8 contains such a positive system.

CHAPTER 5

Middle School Age (8–12 Years)

The educational level for children in this stage of development generally spans third grade to sixth or seventh grade. For many girls, early adolescence begins by age eleven with the onset of menarche (first menstrual period). But today, many girls are experiencing secondary sex characteristics earlier because of several factors, including the presence of growth hormones in various foods in the average American diet. Some girls may experience their first period by age nine or ten. Indeed, it is highly concerning to consider that a child of this age has the biological potential of becoming pregnant and having a baby. Additionally troubling is that a girl this age has not acquired adequate emotional development for parenthood.

Children need education about the imminent physical changes that will occur in puberty. Pediatricians can be a resource and help answer questions or concerns about a child's physical health and development.

I experienced the power of preventative education while participating with a team that presented seminars for eleven-and twelve-year-old boys and girls and their same-sexed parent. Those Friday evening and all-day Saturday seminars provided information about sexuality, healthy relationships, positive self-esteem, and preparing for adolescence.

A female clinician from our team met with the girls, their mothers, and a female staff assistant to cover basic anatomy, physical and emotional changes in puberty, conception, eating disorder prevention, cultural pressure, and abuse prevention that included refusal skills and escape plans. These sessions initiated significant conversations that increased greater understanding and emotional support for these youths.

I met with the boys, their fathers, and a male staff assistant to review the same material with a focus on male anatomy, including a diagram of the bladder, prostate gland, testicles, and penis. Having a staff volunteer present with the clinician during the more in-depth sex education components was part of a safe-child policy.

During the breakout sessions, one of the topics of particular interest was bullying and strategies for seeking help to deal with them in school and the neighborhood. Having the dads present for parts of these breakout sessions was powerful in promoting communication between father and son in these important yet sensitive topics.

While the youths were involved in activity time, our team provided support and additional resources for the parents, including *Sex and the New You* by Richard Bimlar. At the end of the conference, everyone gathered for a community activity and debriefing. I highly recommend you look for opportunities to coordinate with the leadership of your school or church to locate or develop a similar program.

Many excellent resources are available for parents and children. The process of children learning about themselves regarding gender and sexual development starts early in life. Age-appropriate sexual education with positive and accurate information, ideally from the same-sexed parent or designated mentor, is a basic human need. It is particularly critical for this information to be provided prior to the daughter or son experiencing the onset of puberty. It is healthy for parents to be comfortable and supportive when discussing this important topic with their same-sexed child. This part of the parenting job description is often overlooked, but using age-appropriate printed resources are a great aid.

Middle School-Age Development

Let's consider a brief overview of the developmental tasks, psychosocial crisis, and key developmental needs for children in the middle school-age stage of development. The developmental tasks are the following:

- Social cooperation
- Self-evaluation and skill learning
- Team play

Social Cooperation: The Same-Sex Peer Group

From age eight to twelve, we see a significant shift in connecting socially outside the immediate family. These children are receptive to and have a developmentally innate hunger for relationships with others like themselves. Some children with a same-sexed twin, whether identical or fraternal, have a ready-made playmate peer. Eventually, children in this age range have a natural desire to discover peers who are compatible for friendship, which they can find in the neighborhood, school, church, sports team, music organization, etc. We can trace the roots of "peer pressure" and the need for acceptance through conformity to this developmental stage. Early same-sex friendships also form the psychological and relational building blocks for future intimate relationships.[41]

Self-Evaluation and Skill Learning

During this time of life, children give considerable mental energy to evaluating themselves regarding new skills they are learning and mastering. Academic skills, such as reading, interpreting symbols (mathematics), and using language, are the focus of work at this age. Skills also include learning a musical instrument, handwork and crafts, athletics, and other artistic expressions. These skills help the child develop the competencies needed as an adult. A child begins to form evaluations of competencies in these newly acquired skills.[42]

It is, therefore, no wonder that the psychosocial crisis, or tension, for middle school age is "Industry versus Inferiority."[43] As a child's self-concept forms (how they think about themselves) and their self-esteem emerges (how they value themselves), we see the genesis of a trend of thought and perception, which will lean in the direction of either self-confidence or self-doubt. The term *industry* is used to describe the skill-guiding industriousness of children in this age group. *Inferiority* is the risk of a negative self-evaluation compared with peer performance. The Newmans have extended discussion regarding research related to the impact of academic grading systems and "failure messages."

Chapter 10 will cover strategies adults can use to strengthen their self-esteem as imperfect parents. One strategy is to identify your strengths and compensate for your limitations by playing to your strengths. This applies to children too. You can help children survive the storm of self-esteem-crushing influences of others (and the culture) by helping your middle school child identify his or her strengths and aptitudes and not give so much power to areas of limitation and challenge.

Children in this age range often become encyclopedic on any number of topics or hobby interests, such as being able to quote the stats of their favorite sports heroes. Use this opportunity to bond with your child by inviting them to share what they are interested in with you. Of course, you must take the time to listen to and acknowledge what they are sharing with you. Part of supporting their fledgling self-esteem involves giving brief positive feedback. An "atta boy" or "atta girl" will bless them. It is a valuable deposit into their positive confidence bank account.

Team Play

The fourth developmental task for this stage is team play. In the context of play with peers, the child learns what it is to be a member of a team. Team involvement helps a child learn to make a group's goals a higher priority than individual goals. The child learns about the division of labor toward the desired team goal, and the child learns about competition.[44]

Parents and Youth Sports

Think of those overzealous parents at their child's practice or game—those parents who yell technical directions to their child or scold them from the sidelines. This easily becomes a landmine for the child, as it can create confusion about whose direction to follow: the coach's or the forceful parent's (whom they will go home with after the event). The interfering parent may also be over-identifying with their child, perceiving that how well the child performs somehow directly reflects on them as a parent rather than that the child is learning a complicated set of skills. Some parents may be living through the experiences of their children. This can be a result of the parent's history as a high-achieving athlete or not having an opportunity to participate or excel in sports themselves. Regardless of the psychological sources, the child and the team should let the coaches do the coaching. And of course, it is always good to avoid calling out corrective or scolding comments to other members of the child's team, as well. Experienced coaches can appropriately and positively address disruptive behavior and set clear boundaries. We are aware of cases in which a child's love for a particular sport soured due to the parent's excessive scolding and demand for perfection. A pattern of excessive and often public scolding crosses the line into a form of emotional abuse, which is a serious landmine that can have devastating and lasting effects.

CHAPTER 6

Early and Later Adolescence (13–18 years)

My first graduate school course on human growth and development was a pivotal experience. It confirmed my educational path and prepared me for and informed my clinical work with children, adolescents, and their families for years to come. In that growth and development course, I immersed myself in a major research term paper on the life stage of adolescence.

Barbara and Philip Newman expanded Erik Erickson's psychosocial development of adolescence into two critically important stages: early and later adolescence. Another set of theorists, L. Joseph Stone and Joseph Church, also proposed a two-stage theory of early and later adolescence. They developed an eclectic and flexible model for understanding the two stages. Both theories shed light on the biological and social factors that forge the individual who is on the way to becoming an adult. Here are some helpful highlights.

Early Adolescence

Stone and Church view early adolescence as extending from the beginning of the pubescent growth spurt (approximately two years before the onset of puberty and the start of the primary and secondary sex characteristics maturation process) until about one year after the onset of puberty. This is in striking contrast to the Newmans' theory, which suggests that early adolescence lasts until about age eighteen.

For females, the growth spurt occurs on average about two years earlier than their male peers, which can cause them embarrassment if they tower over male peers. The differing maturation rates for males and females can make it difficult for the early adolescent female to wholly accept herself and seek approval from male peers without hiding and minimizing her physical changes.

It can also be challenging for an early adolescent male who experiences a delayed physical growth spurt to see many of his male peers gain height, experience voice change, or grow pubic and facial hair before he does.

"Puberty" is defined as the point at which the individual reaches the biological capacity to reproduce. For females, as mentioned in the previous chapter, the onset of menarche (first menstrual period) on average occurs at approximately age eleven. According to Stone and Church's biologically focused model, this means that pubescence can theoretically start as early as age nine. For males, puberty is indicated by the presence of live spermatozoa cells in the urine at approximately age thirteen. Again, according to Stone and Church, early adolescence for males lasts until somewhere between fourteen and fifteen years of age.

Stone and Church suggest that the individual's search for self-identity is the central psychological theme for both early and later adolescence. Early adolescents are concerned with discovering who they are, including learning about and becoming comfortable with a whole new body and its potential for feeling and behavior while developing a mental picture of self. Thus, the psychosocial crisis for early adolescence is the struggle of "Group Identity versus Alienation," addressing the questions: Who am I, and with whom do I belong?[45]

Youth in this stage have an intensified longing for independence while also seeking peer group acceptance. They possess a drive for increased freedom to follow the dictates of their peer group. One of their primary concerns is their status with significant peers as they strive to be as much like the others as possible, which promotes acceptance by the group. So parents, this innate drive of your early adolescent is developmentally normal.

Our task as parents is to provide a supportive structure to allow positive attachments with peers while preventing the "Lord of the Flies" effect. (*Lord of the Flies* tells the story of a group of young boys marooned on an island after their plane crashes, but without the presence of supportive adults and left to their own devices, this group becomes violent and brutal.) Therefore, I suggest some type of adult supervision, check-in, or accountability for youth through the end of their high school education. Leaving teenagers totally on their own without accountability and support results in "self-parented" youths who are more vulnerable to negative peer influences, including substance use, sexual activity, and gang involvement.

Additionally, we need to sound the call for increased youth mentorship programs, both formal ones like Big Brothers Big Sisters and informal ones. Family members, teachers, coaches, music instructors, and youth group leaders all have opportunities to make a difference in the life of a searching adolescent.

Stone and Church wrote about cross-cultural observations related to rites of passage from childhood to adulthood. Following is a summary of their helpful perspective.

Adolescence as a Cultural Phenomenon

Possibly the most novel and insightful perspective from Stone and Church's theory is their suggestion that the Western European phenomenon of adolescence is a cultural invention and not a universal experience found in all cultures and civilizations. They assert that primitive societies have no equivalent for our concept of adolescence. They look to anthropologists, such as Margaret Mead, who have pointed out that in some cultures, adolescence is not a period of "storm and stress" but is, instead, one of a smooth transition from childhood to adulthood. These same anthropologists have suggested that the physical changes experienced universally by early adolescents are not enough to account for a period of turmoil or "adolescent crisis." Frequently, in more primitive cultures, individuals experience ceremonial adolescence involving puberty rites and initiation, which may range in complexity from a simple haircut or change of clothing to being tattooed, having teeth knocked out, or periodically fasting and staying isolated. Some cultures inflict genital mutilation on females. There are present-day efforts to advocate for discontinuing mutilations. Seldom do these initiation rites last more than a few weeks, and after the ritual, the young person is granted full adult status and assumes it without any sense of stress or conflict.

Stone and Church highlight a key fact that emerges from a comparative study of cultures: The psychological events of adolescence in Western society are not a necessary response to the physical changes of puberty but are a nondeliberate cultural invention produced by an increased postponement of assuming adult responsibilities. Stone and Church observe that as societies become more complex, a time of apprenticeship develops, which separates biological maturity and adulthood. They suggest that extended adolescence is a relatively recent development in Western society. They point to such ceremonies as the Christian confirmation and Jewish Bar Mitzvah and Bat Mitzvah as initially being puberty rites.

They also stress that when adults hesitate to embrace adolescents as young adults, it contributes to adolescents' sense of uncertainty about their identities and roles in society. Common questions are: "What am I going to do with my life?" "Who am I?" "Who or what am I going to become?" This so-called ambiguity is evident as one observes the inconsistency between laws governing adult roles and society's traditional beliefs. In the United States, the legal age for marriage, driving, drinking alcoholic beverages, voting, and participating in the military vary significantly from state to state. Stone and Church admit the complexities of adult life in a modern society like ours demand some type of "apprenticeship," good and constructive support for the emerging young adult. They acknowledge that in modern societies, some conflict between generations may be unavoidable.

The Newmans' Theory of Early Adolescence

The Newmans' psychosocial theory suggests developmental tasks that must be experienced and mastered before a person can successfully enter the stage of later adolescence. These developmental tasks include the following:

- Physical maturation
- Formal cognitive operation, which Piaget contends include thoughts that are directed more by logical principles and learned cause and effect than one's perceptions and experiences
- Membership in a peer group
- Romantic relationships, which are driven by hormones associated with the physical maturation of the reproductive organs

Since we have sufficiently covered early adolescence, we will move on to complete the review of the life stage of later adolescence. We will review helpful material from the psychosocial theory and then conclude this section with considerations from Stone and Church.

Later Adolescence

According to the psychosocial model, one of the identified developmental tasks for a full transition to adulthood is to establish enough autonomy and independence from the parenting unit. Parents can support their seventeen- to twenty-two-year-old in this transition to healthy independence by gradually decreasing the number of restricting rules, encouraging participation in family decision-making, and providing explanations for boundaries and limits (such as necessary house rules).[46] In the college or university environment, you can often spot the folks who are having difficulty making the transition from an overly strict and authoritarian home environment ("You can't do that because I said so") to a less structured environment with more freedom of choices. We do our older adolescents a favor by gradually preparing them to make healthy decisions in a less structured environment resulting in less overt rebellion. This type of parental strategic support promotes the activation of another task: Internalized Morality.

Chapter 5 touched on Lawrence Kohlberg's stages of moral development. Young high school and college-age people show an increased ability to use moral reasoning that involves a commitment to a personal belief system or universal moral value system known as post-conventional moral thinking. Values can be influenced by moral principles, including discussions of situation ethics. Unfortunately, just because someone has the capacity to use higher moral reasoning doesn't mean they will always choose to use it.

Let's revisit the autonomy task. Since the great recession of 2008, more adult children are living with their parents or other relatives than before the recession. Economic and other psychosocial factors can influence the independence and emancipation process. It often makes sense (and cents) for many families to work out arrangements for adult children to live at home. It is important not to take information about developmental tasks, such as the Newmans' focus on autonomy, and make it into a rigid measuring stick of maturity. Extended housing arrangements can present opportunities for financial debt reduction, creative cooperation, and problem-solving for everyone's emotional and financial welfare. "Autonomous-enough" and "significantly independent" may be helpful terms to avoid rigid, all-or-nothing thinking regarding the individuation and emancipation of our adult children.

Another of the Newmans' suggested developmental tasks is the continued reworking of sex-role identification. Adult sex-role identity is shaped by intimate sexual experiences and identification with males or females. Concerning the Newmans' attention to an individual's career choice, an updated perspective would be that males and females can explore and enjoy all career options. Pay discrimination is an example of an economic landmine—many jobs and careers still pay women less than their male counterparts. The other demographic update is that there has been a shift away from career selection that values job loyalty and working up the "corporate ladder" over many years. Present-day young professionals reportedly are willing to move from job to job, motivated to obtain financial and job satisfaction goals in the short-term.

As mentioned earlier, the psychosocial crisis of later adolescence involves resolving individual identity versus role diffusion. For most adolescents, the identity crisis is the product of choices they make about anticipated environmental demands, including the expectations of peers, employers, parents, etc., while preserving the integrity of the individual's developing personality, values, and goals.[47] The identity crisis does not always end with a healthy resolution. Those adolescents who prematurely decide that they will become what family members wish them to become without considering their personality and aspirations experience "identity foreclosure." These young people may be dedicated to their career and other life choices but be out of touch with who they are regarding their potential.[48]

There is a strong argument that accelerated academic track programs requiring high school students to identify and "lock in" their selection of a specific career track may not serve the adolescent's developmental needs. Out of a push for competitive educational achievement and dedicated career path training (for economic efficiency), these programs run the risk of neglecting to give the individual student a well-rounded education. This can potentially set him or her up for a deeper sense of failure if the youth changes tracks and tries something new. It is not unusual for college and university students to change their major area of study multiple times, which normalizes the later adolescent's self-discovery process. This may result in additional time to complete their chosen area of study. Post-high-school college or vocational training programs also provide invaluable personal growth opportunities, regardless of whether or not the economic job markets allow for a paid employment position in that specific field.

Some young people adopt a negative identity by accepting a negative label that society slaps on them. They behave in ways to reinforce the label, much like an internalized self-fulfilling prophecy. One risk of this crisis is role diffusion, which is high on the continuum of interrupted development. The adolescent experiences role diffusion when they are incapable of forming a coherent, single self-view or identity. In other words, they lack a satisfying or stabilizing core identity. When individuals find themselves in a place of developmental "stuck-ness," with resulting symptoms of distress, professional counseling can significantly help. With sensitivity to the individual's values and needs, it is often possible to identify negative life scripts the person may have bought into and then work to replace them with positive truth regarding their tremendous value as a lovingly designed human being.

Professional counseling can significantly contribute to a person's growth in the search for a clearer sense of identity and purpose. Strategic support and cognitive-behavioral therapy techniques that challenge old, distorted messages about self—combined with other supportive therapeutic interventions to help create new neural pathways in the brain—can make a difference in the struggling young adult's quality of life.

Theorists Stone and Church emphasize the need for a society to welcome and accept the transitioning individual to adulthood for their adult role to become a practical reality. Messages of "failure" and "loser," which are forms of emotional abuse, are not constructive in promoting positive core identity formation in our young people.

We need more research and support for identifying factors that empower older adolescents and young adults in our society to possess a greater sense of identity and purpose and for society to extend economic and social acceptance to them as the valued adults they truly are.

Volunteerism and community service contribute to the formation of an adolescent's life, worldview, and sense of purpose in the world. Many schools offer courses that assign and promote various community-service activities. Such leadership is to be applauded, rewarded, encouraged, and duplicated.

As I reflect on character qualities that indicate adult maturity, one that stands out is a good work ethic—fostered and taught through example during early development stages. Responsible adults are valued employees because they follow through on their agreements, do not abandon their post without proper notice, and possess the value of working to provide for their families, even when working under less-than-ideal conditions.

We need a renewed call for positive mentorship. It is vital to the well-being of our young people, young adults, as well as our society to be valued as the precious resources they are. We need parents, teachers, coaches, youth leaders, clergy, and other mentors to not only become enlightened to the developmental needs of our young people but also to respond accordingly. Parents and other mentors who are educated and equipped with child development information have the potential for increasing the numbers of adolescents who make a "healthy enough" transition into adulthood.

PART 3

Developing a Positive Vision for Your Child

CHAPTER 7

Parenting Outcome Goals and Examples of Parenting with a Vision

When parents have a positive vision for their children's character development, it is one of the best gifts a parent can give a child. By guiding with a positive vision, the parent can empower a child to sidestep certain landmines along the road through childhood and adolescence. Such destructive landmines can include seductive voices of outside influence that would seek to undermine the child's sense of unconditional love and acceptance. Insecure adolescents, for example, are vulnerable to chase after the acceptance and approval of their social peer group at any cost.

Develop Your Parenting Vision

We are often more effective in performing a task when we have a mental picture of the end product in our minds. A good example of this is in building a home. If the builder has a detailed plan (blueprint) of what the design of a house, including size, number and placement of rooms, etc., he knows what materials, tools, and subcontractors are required to accomplish the job. Without a plan, the builder is likely to produce an out-of-balance, nonfunctional house that no one can comfortably live in. The job of parenting is a bit like building a house according to blueprints: having a picture of a healthy and thriving future for the child you are raising.

By this I don't mean that the parent is to exert absolute control over how a child develops into a young adult—like the parent whose expectations of a child's career choice overrides the child's interests, talents, skills, passions, and goals. That's an unhealthy approach.

The above scenario serves as a warning of a potential landmine. Excessive control is not necessary for raising children. The artful influence in nurturing and promoting positive character traits in our children is possible. Establishing a strong and healthy foundation upon which our children can build their lives is one of the most loving acts we as parents can do. Acting toward another person in their best interest is a great definition of *love*. Caring parents have the health and well-being of their children at heart. This includes nurturing the child at the developmental stage where they are functioning while not causing the child either to grow up too quickly or be held back from emotionally developing and emancipating at the appropriate time.

In this section, we will look at examples of character traits to either promote or prevent in your child's life. Before we go further, however, I'd like you to stop for a moment and think about the following two key questions:

1. When you picture your child as a young adult, what are the positive character traits and qualities you would like to see being developed in him or her? Write out a list of those qualities that come to mind.

2. In contrast, when you picture your son or daughter as a young adult, what are some of the negative character qualities that you do not want to describe him or her? Write out a list of those characteristics that come to mind.

How did you do? Was this exercise easy or difficult?

You will sometimes hear parents express that they have not wanted to influence their children's belief system so the children can form their own opinions and beliefs without the parents' interference. This mindset is dangerous and makes our children even more vulnerable to society's messages such as these popular ones: "Do it if it feels good," "The one with the most toys [possessions] wins," "Do unto others before they do unto you," "If you've got it, flaunt it," "Might makes right," or "You can do whatever you want if you are large and in charge."

Our children are growing up in a world of predators and prey. The parents who take their job seriously stand as a protective shield against hurtful influences when their children are young and vulnerable. Parents have the opportunity to be empowering launch pads for their emancipating young adults. It is our responsibility to teach our children the necessary values and survival skills that will prepare them to find their way in the world. In this resource-rich era, I encourage parents to access support in the education and character development of their children.

While genetics has a significant influence on human behavior, it is also true that much of human behavior is learned. We parents end up teaching a whole lot more by what we do than what we say. I cannot over-stress the importance of our actions matching our words.

Following is a parallel list of healthy character and behavior traits to promote and unhealthy traits to prevent in our children. The purpose of this list of character traits is to provide a practical target in character development as you raise your child. Feel free to draw from it as you develop your personal list:

Healthy traits to promote	Unhealthy traits to prevent
1. Growing and thriving	At significant risk of disease and early death
2. Secure and confident with a healthy sense of self-esteem and identity as a loved and valued human being	Insecure; given to self-doubt; confusion related to personal identity; self-condemnation
3. Accepts responsibility for own actions and choices	Blames others for own mistakes (blame-shifting)
4. Willing to work hard for needs and wants (strong work ethic)	An attitude of entitlement: others owe him/her a comfortable life; or the opposite extreme: "work-a-holism," which is excessive work to avoid/neglect life outside out of work
5. Free from addictions (in recovery)	Addicted to mood-altering substances, gambling, shopping, eating disorders, rage, pornography, sex, abusive relationships, power and control, materialism, or other excessive behaviors that lead to impaired functioning or neglect of self or relationships
6. Free from abuse; able to recover from hurts with support	Continually views self as a victim of life (victim mentality); seeing others as a perpetrator

7. Demonstrates an active conscience; knows the difference between right and wrong; consistently a truth-teller; honest in business	Consistently given to lying and deception; lack of remorse when hurting another person or animal
8. Compassionate for other people and takes action, such as sharing resources	Selfish greed for money and material possessions; lack of empathy; driven by a lust for power in decisions and behavior
9. Law-abiding and respectful of authority	Consistently behaves as though laws do not apply to him or her (above the law)
10. Productive employee; effective in teamwork	"Allergic" to hard work; expects others to do his or her work
11. Demonstrates good "survival skills"; has healthy boundaries; allows others to prove their trustworthiness—not blind loyalty	Too easily trusts those who misuse power to exploit or take advantage; vulnerable to negative influences of others
12. Accepting of all people as equal in value as human beings	Judgmental, prejudiced, racist, or unaccepting of people with differences of opinion
13. Monogamous, faithful	Infidelity; unable to commit; involvement in multiple intimate relationships simultaneously
14. Problem-solve through non-violent methods; behaving like a person of peace	Bullying and intimidation; verbal and physical violence; teaching violence by example
15. Respectful of members of the opposite sex as valued people, not as objects	Disrespectful; exploitive; manipulating others without consideration of their feelings

16. Able to ask for and receive forgiveness for mistakes and offenses toward others; able to give forgiveness to others who have intentionally or unintentionally committed offenses against him or her	Unable to ask for or accept forgiveness for offending others; unforgiveness toward others who have hurt, disrespected, or exploited him or her; holds on to grudges, resentment, and hatred

Keep reviewing and developing your personal list of target traits. It's about consistent trends in behavior, not perfection.

But what if, after reviewing this list, you've identified a few traits within yourself that fall on the Unhealthy Traits to Prevent side? Just as our kids aren't perfect, we aren't either. However, if some significant unhealthy items are challenges for you, I encourage you to reach out to a qualified professional who can help you address these issues that could interfere with your effective parenting. Please review the variety of resources listed at the back of this book.

Consider #16 on the previous list: "Able to ask for and receive forgiveness for mistakes and offenses toward others; able to give forgiveness to others who have intentionally or unintentionally committed offenses against him or her." Many adults have not learned the language, attitude, and behavior of forgiveness. What better place to model the giving and receiving of forgiveness than in our homes. It serves as a powerful teaching tool in raising children who are able to give and receive forgiveness.

In the next section, we will consider practical examples of applying a positive vision, including strategies for promoting bonding, character development, and faith formation.

Examples of Parenting with a Vision

Now that you have begun to picture a positive future (vision) for your child, we will consider options for applying that vision in your intentional parenting at different stages of your child's development.

During Pregnancy

Parenting with a vison can start while the little one is in the secret room of the mother's womb. Bonding is promoted when the pregnant mom takes time to sit down, relax, take slow deep breaths, and reflect on the joy of having this baby in her life, now, in this moment, and in the future. Periodically take time to visualize a secure and happy child. You can use visual props such as the latest ultrasound image. You could also turn to the picture on page one of Chapter One of this book. Picture your little one warm and cozy, and marvel at the Creator's design. Taking time to relax in this way also helps support your self-care with intentional times of lowered stress. Dads can also participate in times of welcoming relaxation. Talking and singing to the developing child also promote bonding and the message of loving welcome.

During Infancy

Sleep disruption. Sleep deprivation. Low energy. Sick baby. Physical and emotional exhaustion. These can be part of the experience with newborns. Often, survival is the goal. Practice self-compassion. When you are able, remember to smile into the face of your baby. Speak words of reassurance to her. Find ways to be her cheerleader, celebrating accomplishments and soothing her disappointments. It may be that the best time to practice gratitude is when the bundle of joy is finally asleep. The picture of peace, or exhaustion, depending on the day. This may be the best time to lift up prayers of gratitude and thankfulness. Keep reminding yourself your infant will most likely not always be as dependent on you as she is right now.

During Childhood

Character development in children is complex with many contributing factors. There are individual personality factors, genetics, and environmental influences. Environmental factors include such things as a loving and consistently secure home and the negative impacts of trauma, loss, and neglect.

It's not about raising a perfect child but about developing their character first so that healthy (godly) behavior naturally becomes more consistent over time. Model behaviors you desire to see cultivated in your child.

Colossians 3:12–13 describes a wardrobe of virtues we are to put on like clothing: compassion, kindness, humility, gentleness, patience. To forgive one another and to put on love, which binds these virtues together in "perfect unity."

As a parent of a young child, you will have opportunities to contribute to the development of your child's conscience. To teach right from wrong. To begin to imagine the feelings of another person and to care about another's well-being. This aspect of character development ties into the previous discussion of moral development in part 2, chapter 4. These are the formative years when a child's conscience is activated. Be ready to look for opportunities for life lessons.

It is also wise to teach honesty and healthy boundaries in childhood, to prevent people-pleasing tendencies. People pleasing can include not being honest with our own feelings and needs. The person is focused on the approval of others to the neglect of their own needs. They can lose a sense of their own identity. It is healthy for a child to have a sense of who they are as a person, having a distinct reality separate from others around them.

A note of warning of a potential landmine when teaching the qualities of generosity and sharing possessions [toys, clothing, etc.] with other children: Do not expect or pressure a young child to voluntarily give away a beloved toy or item to another child in need. Children develop compassion at different paces. To force a child to donate a beloved item would cause hurt and resentment, as she would feel her item was taken unfairly. Allow the child to consider donating items for the needs of other children when they are emotionally ready. There may be opportunities for the child to learn to share toys with visiting friends when they are old enough to tolerate it and understand it is not a permanent exchange.

Photos of your child can be used as a visual aid as you pray God's blessing on your child's present and future. Allow yourself to trust that God has positive hopes and dreams for your child. This is a powerful anchor to hold onto when life's storms rage and the future is uncertain.

Let your light shine with your children. Use opportunities throughout the day to demonstrate God's love to them, and model gratitude for God's provision and loving care in many creative ways. Offering thanks at mealtimes is an example of integrating your faith into family routines. Many wonderfully illustrated children's Bible storybooks are available for child-oriented family devotions and evening reading times. There is also a variety of quality children's books and videos that teach virtues and encourage faith formation.

A note of warning of a potential landmine in faith formation with people of any age—particularly with children: Avoid the use of fear or guilt to promote faith. This can cause a trauma wound. A fear-based faith or a shame-based faith may have short-term response. Focus on God's unconditional love and acceptance and his provision for forgiving the worst of our mistakes. Faith grounded in love and trust has staying power that lasts a lifetime—and beyond.

Bedtime prayers with your child have the potential of becoming a special and meaningful part of the bedtime routine. As a parent becomes more comfortable praying out loud with and for the prever-bal child, the child will eventually, in turn, be able to express their prayers more easily. Talking together with God at the end of the day can be a blessing with many benefits to both the child and the parent. Verbalizing words of thanks, asking for help, and praying for bless-ings for others can be a calming and stress-releasing experience that promotes restful sleep for the child . . . and for the parent. Sharing and teaching your trust in the Lord with your child not only gives your child a gift that will serve her well throughout life but also may surprise you with the unexpected blessing of increased spiritual growth for yourself. Incorporating faith into your family's lifestyle can be a beautiful way to apply the direction for parents found in Deuteronomy 6:5–7:

Love the Lord your God with all your heart and with all your soul and with all your strength. These commandments that I give you today are to be upon your hearts. Impress them on your children. Talk about them when you sit at home and when you walk along the road [or go for a ride in the car], when you lie down and when you get up.

During Adolescence

It is important for early and later-aged adolescence to know they are a priority to the parent. Taking time for planned parent-child activities sends a positive message louder than any verbal declaration of love and appreciation. The verbal expressions of heartfelt caring are also important. Give of your time. Don't be dissuaded by your adolescence's hesitancy or resistance. Find out what activities they would be willing to do with you. Are they willing to go for a day hike? A bike ride? Go to a concert? Have lunch together? Play a favorite game just the two of you? Once you get a "yes," mark it on the calendar and follow through. Be consistent with keeping your commitments to your child at the same level of priority you would give a business client.

Character development with an adolescent could include volunteering together at some community service. This opens up creative possibilities. There may be opportunities again in the future to participate in a domestic or international service-oriented mission trip together. What an amazing activity for appreciating what we have (gratitude) and gaining greater appreciation of other cultures (compassion).

Anger is a factor in character development in adolescence. How do you model anger? Especially when you passionately believe you support the most morally just political candidate, party, religious denomination, or cause. How do you handle differences of opinion? Modeling humility includes being teachable, being able to appreciate something in another person's differing point of view and to not presume to have the last word of wisdom. When your adolescent witnesses your efforts to be fair and reasonable, not rigid and dogmatic, it is more likely your personal values and opinion will be heard and respected. When family members hear each other clearly, it leads to greater understanding. Greater understanding can lead to greater empathy, despite differences of opinion.

May this section be a catalyst for your personal reflection and growth in your parenting journey. In the next chapter, we will consider strategies for correction and discipline when limits need to be set.

PART 4

A Positive Approach to Discipline

CHAPTER 8

A New Perspective

The previous section established that it is the parent's responsibility to teach the child right from wrong, discipline, and reasonable limits. If the parent fails to introduce an intentional value system to train the child to respect self, others, and others' possessions, the child will adopt someone else's value system. That value system will most likely be the one modeled and taught by example. The value system a child internalizes in such a non-directed environment could put them at high risk of engaging, for example, in antisocial behaviors for the sake of self-gratification. Without healthy discipline and self-control, the child, family, and ultimately society suffer. This is one reason laws exist that make parents legally responsible for their children's behavior until the child becomes eighteen years old. Teaching self-discipline to children is a vital part of the parenting job description.

In my twenty-nine years of clinical work with children and adolescents, I've found that children who have experienced emotional, physical, or sexual trauma often have a heightened need for control over their bodies. They need to control who touches their body and how and where touching occurs. A system of discipline that does not rely on corporal punishment is most appropriate for a child with a trauma history. If a system of discipline that does not involve physical punishment or the fear of shame can be highly effective with children who have a trauma history, why not use such a system with all children?

I encourage you to review the system of discipline that follows and evaluate its logical consistency and strengths. Nonphysical punishment approaches to discipline bring out the best in a parent, and, in the long run, also in a child. The *Webster's New Collegiate Dictionary* definition of *discipline* is: "to train or develop by instruction; training that connects, molds or perfects the mental faculties of moral character; self-control; a rule or system of rules governing conduct."

The system of discipline outlined in this section requires that children have the cognitive ability to understand the parents' requests and that they are old enough to have at least some control over their bodies. Therefore, it can be adopted for children ranging from two-and-a-half years through seventeen years of age. It is not appropriate for infants under the age of two because they do not have the cognitive development or physical impulse control to be disciplined with consequences. Infants and young children lacking impulse control need the security of a child-proofed environment in which potentially dangerous objects have been removed or blocked from access.

The system of discipline presented here is instrumental in helping children develop internal controls and the ability to use impulse control. It is a powerful tool in teaching children about forgiveness when they make mistakes. This system also helps activate the child's conscience, which is their internal sense of right and wrong.

House Rules

The foundation of this life-giving system is a balanced and updated list of the parents' house rules. It is always easier for parents to focus on behaviors that are *not* allowed rather than desired behaviors. Children and adolescents need to have a clear, positive target of what is okay. The following is an example of a list of balanced house rules that is not too long or overly detailed. Feel free to adapt this for personal use. Use the blanks to add any house ground rules. For example, some children may need it spelled out to ask for parents' permission before inviting friends to stay overnight or to stay for dinner at the family home.

Okay	Not okay
Gentle hugs and appropriate touch with permission	Hitting, kicking, biting, or other physical harm
Honest, polite, and kind speech to others	Yelling, swearing, name calling, put-downs, or lying
Waiting your turn	Interrupting
Listening to and following parents' directions Expressing what may not feel fair respectfully	Ignoring or refusing parents' directions
Non-alcoholic beverages Respecting the legal drinking age	Illegal drugs, alcohol use, or abuse of prescription medications
Respecting others' property Asking for permission before using someone else's things	Stealing or using others' things without asking permission

Family Meeting

Once parents have agreed on a list of balanced house rules, it is time to schedule a family meeting to review it with the child verbally. Children of any age will benefit from special emphasis on the "okay" list. Be creative! A brief demonstration or role-playing of selected key items can create a memorable impression. This family meeting serves as an illustrated notice for the child—she has now been informed of the behavioral expectations. Feel free to implement the system of discipline provided later in the chapter. Please understand that it will take a child (and parent) up to a couple of months to feel comfortable with a new system, especially in situations where new rules or boundaries have been added to the house rules. Look for opportunities to give your child a chance to pull unacceptable behavior back into line.

Let's apply this system to the following common tech-toy scenario:

You gave your seven-year-old child the routine notice that he has five minutes left to play. After three minutes, you gave a two-minute notice of time left to play the game. At the end of the two minutes, you followed up by calmly directing your child that the two minutes is over and that it's time to turn off the game. Your son yells in angry protest. You respond by lowering the volume of your voice, calling your child by name, and saying something like, "I want you to calm down and take a deep breath. Show me. Breathe in. Now blow it out. Thanks." As your child starts to breathe normally, you continue: "Use your words when you are frustrated. I understand you want to play the game longer. You need to stop now because the amount of playtime we agreed on is used up for today. If you show me you can keep our agreement without arguing, then you'll be able to play some more tomorrow after your schoolwork is done. Thank you for calming down." Then you say with a calm and encouraging voice, "What's the rule about yelling?" If your child is able to summarize the house rule ("no yelling"), you have succeeded in being "the good guy" by helping your child to get his behavior under control. You have helped to prevent the need for drawn-out confrontation and consequences.

Parents need to anticipate that a child will likely protest to some degree when directed to stop a favorite activity and move to a new task (at least at first). Adopting realistic expectations help parents manage their parenting-related stress more effectively. Remember to give the child who has cooperated immediate verbal praise to reinforce the positive choice. For example, "Thank you for remembering the rule about not yelling. It feels really good when you use your words with respect. I'm very proud of you." Now the child is likely more receptive to redirecting from the video game to the next activity. For younger children, it is helpful to have a plan for a positive next step after the video game time.

Now that you have held the family meeting with illustrations of your house rules, the stage is set for implementing the system of discipline. The outlined system is appropriate for use when a house rule is repeatedly violated, when there is a one-time violation that requires a strong response, or when another person's rights have been violated. For two-parent households, designate one parent as the spokesperson when both parents are present. The spokesperson handles communication with the child for that specific incident from start to finish. This approach promotes unity in the parenting team and prevents the risk of "splitting" or disagreement between the parents. It is best for both parents to take turns being the spokesperson. This format is instrumental in training the child to respect both the mother and father's parental authority. In single-parent households, you will have many opportunities to shape your child's inner voice of conscience. In foster families who have young children with neglect or abuse histories, the parent should sit in the same room for the brief "time-out" incorporated in the following system because time-outs of separation or isolation can trigger abandonment reactions in children with these histories and issues.

A System of Discipline Everyone Can Live With

Step 1: Confrontation

"I need you to come with me and have a seat." (Choose a neutral place but not in the child's room.)

"Your mistake was that you _____
_____."

Step 2: First time-out

"I need you to sit here and think about your mistake, and when I come back, I want you to tell me what your mistake was."

The length of this time-out is thirty seconds to three minutes, depending on the child's age and attention span.

For young or impulsive children, parents should sit near the child during the time-out.

Step 3: Confession

"Thank you for sitting for the time-out."

The parent spokesperson then asks the child, "What was your mistake?"

This is to activate the young child's conscience and the encourage the older child to take ownership (responsibility) for their behavior.

If the child takes responsibility by verbalizing the original mistake, the parent should respond by saying, "Thank you for telling me your mistake" and move on to step 4.

If the child refuses to verbalize or write out the original mistake, the parent should respond, "It looks like you need a few more minutes to sit and think about your mistake." The parent should then restate the original mistake (step 1) and repeat step 2 with a brief time-out. Parents must be willing to "outlast" the child by requiring a reasonable level of admission of responsibility without raging at or shaming the child. If the child refuses or is unable to state their mistake verbally, parents should provide options for the child, including letting them write out a description of what they did or point to the violated house rule. Only proceed to the next step when step 3 is completed.

Step 4: Second Time-Out

The parent should now state, "Now I want you to sit for a couple of minutes [the same length of time as first time-out] to think of a positive job you can do." A constructive and non-shaming chore or task is similar to "community service," contributing back to the family community while rebuilding the child's self-esteem after being "humbled."

Step 5: Huddle

Now the parent should ask, "What ideas do you have for a positive job?"

It is fine to incorporate the child's ideas. The task is most effective when it is age-appropriate and takes approximately one to two minutes for every year of the child's emotional age. For example, a good job for a seven-year-old impulsive or immature child would take ten minutes. The task should not be directly related to the original mistake. If the original mistake created a mess, it is best for the parent to help the young child clean up the mess after the last step of the system of discipline. This helps to avoid shaming her. It is also good to remember that accidents happen—so treat an accident differently from an intentional rule violation. An accident that does not hurt someone else does not require discipline.

Step 6. Positive Job

Give clear direction to the child on the assigned task—the positive job. Include directions for how you want the job done and your expectations for the end result. This is especially important when the task is new to the child. The goal is to set the child up for success, not failure or misunderstanding.

To give directions for a positive job, go with the child to their bedroom and state the instructions in a calm and firm voice: "Your positive job is to pick up all of the toys on the floor in this room and put them away on the shelves where they belong." Point to the shelves or toy box where you want the toys to end up.

Use a timer with a bell or buzzer to signal when the time for the positive job is over. For example, set twenty minutes for folding clean towels. When assigning weeding in the flower bed as an age-appropriate positive job, be sure to clearly identify for the child which ones are the weeds to be pulled and which ones are the plants to be left alone.

Step 7: Rejoin and Review

Have the child alert you (or the caregiver) when they have finished the positive job. The parent should respond, "Show me what you did."

Inspect the task. If it is incomplete, the parent states to the younger child in an encouraging tone of voice, "Do you need me to help you finish, or can you finish this part yourself?" Regarding an older child/adolescent, the parent does well to acknowledge the child's effort and encourage completing the task. For example, the parent could say, "Looks like a good start. Please finish this section like how we talked about it. Come and get me when you're done." When the child completes the positive job, praise them for their work. "Thank you. You did a good job!"

Step 8: Forgiveness

Bend down so that you are eye level with your child and hug them. While holding them, say those powerful words: "I forgive you." If the original mistake involved harm to another person or destruction of property, make a plan for the child to make amends and any age-appropriate restitution (including financial payment). Once the original mistake is forgiven and done with, do not bring it up again. This will prevent unforgiveness and shaming. Work through multiple significant mistakes one at a time, going through steps 1–7 for each one (within reason and according to the child's development level and ability).

How It Works

In the real world of family life, situations may arise that require customized consequences. This could include "natural consequences," such as a time-limited restriction of an adolescent's driving privileges for a serious violation of the house rules involving the family car. Parents will develop the ability to determine when it is appropriate to use natural consequences as part of the reasonable discipline.

When an underage youth is involved in using alcohol or other controlled substances, it may be appropriate to require a substance use disorder evaluation with a professionally trained and qualified evaluator. The benefits of specialized and thorough evaluation include the following:

- The youth will hear from another adult that substance use is illegal and carries the risk of legal consequences if the substance use continues.
- This experience can help prevent further incidents of substance use.
- The youth will receive a comprehensive evaluation that identifies if the substance use was an isolated incident or meets the criteria for a substance use disorder.

- The caregiver can deal with the seriousness of the substance use without participating in ineffective or destructive behaviors, such as shaming, belittling, screaming, physical violence, or grounding for life.

It is of extreme importance that parents demonstrate that they are ready, willing, and able to back up their words with reasonable consequences. This is not so that children will be afraid of us. Rather, it is to believe us—that we mean what we say.

Don't threaten a consequence you never would or are not able to act on. Threats of violence or abandonment break the child's sense of security and trust. Remember, fear is not an effective motivator for long-term change or compliance. It is important to stay flexible. Don't paint yourself into a corner. If you respond to your child's bad behavior in the heat of the moment with extreme and severe consequences, pause, reflect, and calm down before acting on your words. It is powerful for your child to watch you taking a time-out to calm yourself and consider a more reasonable consequence. As children mature, they have an increased developmental and emotional need for consequences to be fair. A straightforward script for changing to a more reasonable course is, "We changed our minds. Our original decision was more severe than necessary. This is what we have decided: _____."

A Discipline Landmine to Avoid

Perhaps these words uttered by a frustrated parent (perhaps from our own mouth) sound familiar: "You just wait 'til your father gets home!" This communicates to the child that one parent has more authority than the other.

In a two-parent household, with mother and father, the child needs to be trained to respect both parents' authority. When the mother relies on the father, stepfather, or another male parenting figure as the disciplinarian or enforcer, potential risks include:

- The male figure disliking and potentially resenting the enforcer role.

- The male figure applying excessively harsh and severe treatment of the child due to built-up stress, anger, or resentment.
- The child being conditioned not to look forward to the adult's return home.
- The child being conditioned to expect that Mom doesn't have the authority or power to give discipline consequences and decisions, leading to an undermining of the child's respect for Mom's role.
- The child's distorted perception that Mom is not deserving of the same degree of respect as the parent with the "power".
- Mom reinforcing the message that her words do not carry the same importance as her man and feeling powerless or less than competent to manage the child's behavior.

I empathize with the single parent who does not have the support or "back up" of another parenting team member in the home. Single parents can expand their support system for dealing with the demands of parenting by joining a parents' group, establishing friendships with other parents, and locating a professional family counselor. It is vital to be connected to a supportive community while performing this highly challenging and stressful job.

I also encourage single parents to put intentional energy into a lifestyle of whole-person wellness and self-care. Such a lifestyle may include scheduled physical activity, rest, staying hydrated, balanced nutrition, respite childcare support for needed breaks, social and spiritual contacts for encouragement, and balanced nutrition. It's not far off from the training regimen of an Olympic athlete. Parents will have more to give their children when they make self-care a priority. Consider the mom of a newborn who takes a nap when the baby is sleeping. Making self-nurture a priority is like the emergency instructions that flight attendants give: "Put on your own oxygen mask before assisting your child with his." If the parent doesn't put her mask on first, she will pass out and be of no help to her child. Similarly, a parent will have more energy for the child when the parent is adequately nourished, healthy, and supported.

Discipline

As previously discussed, Barbara M. Newman and Philip R. Newman have done a marvelous job discussing human development organized around ten life stages. The Newmans review research studies regarding discipline styles in the chapter entitled "Toddlerhood" in their book *Development Through Life*. They begin the review of discipline techniques with the observation that toddlers' natural perception of the world is that they are at the center of everything. This egocentric view of life—combined with physical excitability and impulsivity—sets up the toddler to be in conflict with his parents. The ideal goal, then, is for parental discipline to help toddlers achieve confidence in their ability to control their behavior without extreme fear of parental anger or rejection.[49]

The Newmans summarize foundational research related to discipline practices and techniques. Human nature is consistent over time. While social, cultural, and economic contexts can change from generation to generation, the core elements of child development remain consistent. So, too, are the basic categories into which parents' discipline styles fall.

Grace-Based versus Shame-Based Discipline

Grace-based parenting describes an approach in which the parent communicates through actions and verbal statements consistent with a position of acceptance of the child as a valued person whose identity is not diminished by behavior mistakes.[50] Shaming, even if unintended, communicates that the individual not only made a mistake but that he *is* a mistake.

In his article, "Consequences of Different Kinds of Parental Discipline," in *Review of Child Development Research*, Wesley Becker observes that parental discipline can be generally categorized in three continuums: warmth/hostility, restrictiveness/permissiveness, and calm detachments/anxious emotional involvement. The Newmans highlight the helpfulness of this model by comparing the overly protective parent and the organized, effective parent. Both discipline styles are high on warmth and restrictiveness, yet the overprotective parent tends to be more anxious and emotionally involved. The organized, effective parent tends to be calmer and more responsive while still caring.[51]

In addition to Becker, Martin Hoffman has written on research related to the impact of parents' discipline techniques on their children's behavior and moral development. Following is a brief summary of Hoffman's helpful findings.

Discipline practices can be broken down into two main categories: (1) power-assertive discipline and (2) psychological discipline. Power-assertive approaches include physical punishment, shouting, threats of punishments, physically moving the child to another location, or removing an object (like a breakable glass vase) from the child's sight and reach.

Psychological discipline can be further separated into (1) love withdrawal and guilt and (2) age-appropriate explanations of consequences of the child's behavior for herself, other family members, or others in the community. These explanations and consequences may include suggestions and direction regarding more appropriate options for responding to a situation.

These strategies, as part of discipline, are more likely to help promote empathy, the ability to put oneself into the shoes of another person and connect with their feelings, and activate the child's conscience to discern cause and effect. Parental modeling and positive reinforcement of acceptable behavior are key factors in the child's internal control development—that is, the child's learned ability to put on behavioral brakes. A child needs to know what is appropriate to avoid unacceptable behavior.[52]

This is why the System of Discipline Everyone Can Live With includes the balanced list of house rules. It is a matter of when, not if, our children will make mistakes. As parents, we must not discipline out of frustration and anger, which can lead to excessive physical force. Also, we should avoid destructive psychological discipline, which uses guilt-tripping and love withdrawal.

Following this system and its suggested structure and plan for reasonable discipline empowers the caregiver to discipline with confidence. It helps prevent stepping on the landmines of toxic control, including physically and psychologically coercive and harsh tactics that are better left for use in military boot camp to train adults for combat.

Our actions are the most powerful form of communication with our children. Remember, they learn more from what we do than what we say. When we consistently show through our words and actions that we value and accept them—even when they make a serious or repeated mistake—we nurture and strengthen healthy emotional and moral development. The Bible encourages this kind of discipline:

Children, do what your parents tell you. This is only right.... Fathers, don't frustrate your children with no-win scenarios. Take them by the hand and lead them in the way of the Master. (Ephesians 6:1, 4 MSG)

Train up a child in the way he should go, and when he is old he will not turn from it. (Proverbs 22:6 NKJV)

Parents don't come down too hard on your children or you'll crush their spirits. (Colossians 3:21 MSG)

CHAPTER 9

Removing Anger from Discipline

A key principal of effective discipline is to intentionally manage our own anger intensity to respond rationally to stressful discipline situations. Increased self-awareness is the key. When we operate with a low degree of self-awareness, we are at higher risk of reacting out of hurt, fatigue, frustration, or rage.

The information and skills presented in this chapter are designed to help you understand and access the basic principles of crisis management. By practicing these skills, you will become more confident and effective in your discipline skills and parenting overall. This includes strategies for increasing self-awareness of emotions, personal space dynamics, skills for calming yourself and diffusing your child's anger, and strategies for responding to threats of violence.

Start with a short quiz to explore the degree to which anger has been a part of your discipline practices. The quiz will help you identify if excessive anger has been part of your discipline. To promote honesty and privacy in this exercise, make a mental note of your responses without marking the page with your answers.

1. I have used harsh physical punishment in anger or rage while disciplining my child two or more times. (This can include

slapping, pinching, or spanking with more physical force than intended.)

Yes / No

2. I react quickly to a discipline situation with physical punishment before I have gathered complete information regarding the details of who did what.

Seldom/Never   Sometimes   Frequently

3. I have slapped, spanked, or whipped a child after deciding not to use these methods.

Yes No

4. I have experienced recurring thoughts of anger. For example, "The child 'deserves to feel it hurt' because their behavior broke or damaged something of value, hurt my feelings, or defied my parental authority."

Yes No

5. I believe I am justified in delivering a blistering spanking to my child to fulfill my position of authority in my home.

Yes No

6. A significant other or another person close to me has asked me to stop using physical punishment because of past incidents of excessive harshness (as measured by the significant other).

Yes No

7. I have brought up a past offense that has already been addressed with consequences and verbally scolded or shamed my child again for it.

Yes No

Review your answers. A yes answer to any of these questions is a red flag. Please do not ignore these symptoms of excessive anger while disciplining your child. Bringing up previously resolved offenses is shaming and may indicate that the parent has difficulty letting go or forgiving an offense and may hold onto grudges. They might need professional counseling regarding any items that are severe or are a repeated tendency or pattern.

Knowing what kinds of behavioral problems and rule violations push your buttons is important. Identifying types of situations that trigger anger can help prevent this particular landmine and empower you to be more effective in your child's discipline.

The Irrational Zone

Emotions are not logical. However, many emotions occur for good reasons—with rational causes. For example, it makes sense that a person would experience shock, fear, confusion, and anger if they had just experienced an unprovoked, violent physical attack. The person would want information regarding the reason and motive behind the assault: "Why me? Was it planned or impulsive? What did I ever do to that person to justify that kind of attack? Was it random?"

Strong emotions can have clear, underlying causes. Emotions can also be driven by changes in a person's hormonal levels or brain chemistry. For example, Alzheimer's disease can cause involuntary outbursts of anger like yelling profanities contrary to the person's behavior and personality prior to the onset. Strong emotions can also be a secondary reaction to a person's perceptions—how things appear. If a person lacks all the facts regarding a situation, they may feel they are being treated unfairly and therefore experience emotional pain, betrayal, discouragement, anger, resentment, or rage. It is crucial to check out and test perceptions and learn more about a situation rather than jumping to a hasty conclusion.

Every human being has the potential for crossing over into the irrational zone, where a person becomes emotionally—even for a moment—irrational, illogical, or unreasonable. The person in the irrational zone no longer listens to new information regarding another point of view or concerns. The autonomic nervous system kicks in with increases in adrenalin and heart rate, with blood rushing from the brain to the muscle groups ready for fight, flight, or freeze. The anger reaction can escalate physical agitation, voice volume, and animated facial expressions. In essence, the irrational zone takes control of the interaction and cuts off further constructive discussion. Intensified feelings and perceptions can include feeling unheard, unvalued, dismissed, or disrespected, which can result in a verbal attack stemming from the pain of that perception.

Personal Space Bubble

The term "personal space bubble" refers to the amount of space a person needs to have between themself and another person to feel comfortable in any given social contact.

A fun exercise for a small group is to form two lines on opposite sides of a room, each person facing someone they are not related to. At the signal, the people in each line begin to walk toward the person across from them slowly. Each person is instructed to stop and stand in place when they reach their limit of comfortable distance. Any closer and they would not feel comfortable. When one person stops, the person across from them stops too. Then with permission, the other person continues walking closer to demonstrate *their* comfort zone. Some people are comfortable with a close space. Others need a larger personal space bubble to feel comfortable. Gender, age, culture, and familiarity may be factors impacting a person's space bubble.

With the concept of personal space bubble, another piece of information might be helpful. A personal space bubble widens when stress, tension, or conflict increases between the individuals facing each other. This is as true for the child as it is for the parent.

When people feel smothered, confronted, or threatened by another who is physically too close, they might say, "Get out of my face!" or "I need space." An assertive script for requesting more space could be something like, "I'm feeling uncomfortable with how close we are standing. I need to take a few steps back to feel more comfortable."

For this reason, wise responses to an individual who is agitated and becoming enraged include stepping back or leaning against or sitting on a counter, desk, table, or the arm of a chair. (Sitting too low can make a person feel vulnerable, while these slightly elevated postures prepare a person for self-defense and express authority.) Alternatively, you can encourage the distressed person to go outside for some fresh air or allow them to leave the room. All these options create a more spacious and calming personal space bubble.

Talk-Down Skills

A person does not have to be trained as an FBI negotiator to learn and effectively use "talk-down skills." One of the most important steps in talking someone down is being aware of your own frustration and anger level. It is always better and more effective to take a quick "self-check-in" and manage your emotions before attempting to manage someone else's. Otherwise, you run the risk of reacting poorly, escalating (rather than diffusing) the situation, and crossing into the irrational zone yourself.

First, ask yourself (on an anger scale of one to ten, with ten being the highest): What is my anger level right now? Then, take the following self-coaching steps:

- If your anger level is eight or higher, give yourself a moment to bring it down to seven or lower. (You are now modeling the self-coaching behavior you want your child or adolescent to learn for themselves.)
- Take a slow, deep breath—in through the nose and slowly out through the mouth.
- Start self-talk—like, "I am pretty angry right now. I need to breathe and calm down so I can help ＿＿＿＿＿＿ calm down" or "I need to be the rational adult in the situation."

Self-talk is best done silently or whispered as quietly as possible. Once your anger and frustration level are under control, you're ready for the next step in "talking down" an out-of-control child, adolescent, or adult. This should not come across demeaning or condescending to another person, such as "talking down *to*" someone else. Instead, talking down means coaching a person from a high degree of agitation, anger, fear, or confusion down to a place of increased calm and decreased distress and reactivity. Agitation is a blend of anxiousness (fear) and irritability (anger).

The goal of talking someone down in such an emotional state is diffusing their escalation by calmly yet firmly directing them using words to help them calm down, breathe, and regain positive self-control. First, say the person's first name in a calm, firm voice. Then, initiate two important steps to de-escalate them from the irrational zone:

1. Move into the person's field of vision so they can see you. For sight-impaired individuals, move close enough so they can clearly hear you when talking in a firm, calm voice.
2. Respect their personal space bubble by allowing moderate space. For example, if their typical personal space bubble when calm is two-and-a-half feet, increase that to at least six to eight feet when agitated. This helps to prevent them from escalating to hitting, kicking, or biting.

Here is an example of a script to talk down a fictitious girl, Yvonne, who has crossed into the irrational zone:

"Yvonne, we need to calm down."

"Look at my eyes, Yvonne."

"Right now, Yvonne, we just need to calm down."

"I want you to breathe with me. Take a breath in—through the nose. Now blow it out through your mouth. Good. Let's do that again. Breathe in. Now blow out. Very good, Yvonne."

"Right now, Yvonne, I want you to calm down."

"Yes, Yvonne, we can talk about it later. We will come up with a solution later."

"Yvonne, I can hear you better when you are not yelling."

"Okay, Yvonne, let's take another breath together. Good job! Can you start to feel yourself becoming more relaxed?"

The above sentences should be short statements with pauses. Slow the pace of your words. Use your voice as a coaching tool to help the person calm down and regain control, which is the singular, immediate task. For the time being, let go of the issue that led to the escalation. The first priority is to intervene and help them regain control through breathing and support.

This is not the time to discuss the consequences for whatever house rule they have violated. Nor is it the time to debate or argue the issue that triggered the meltdown. You will have plenty of time later to sort out the details. Remember, it is impossible to discuss the issue—much less resolve it—until both parties are rational (able to listen to the other person without a verbal attack or tirade). Only when cooler heads prevail will you be able to move forward. Until then, your job is to work with the other person to calm them down and help them regain appropriate control.

Responding to Threats of Violence

As a child gets older (and bigger), temper tantrums can morph into threats of violence, destruction of property, and assaultive behavior—and the risk of injury and destructive habits may also increase. The disciplinary intervention described in A System of Discipline Everyone Can Live With may not eliminate threatening behavior in your child or teenager. In such cases, you should take threats of violence and assaultive behavior seriously.

At the first observation of violent threats or assaultive behavior at home, at school, or in the neighborhood, your child or teen should be evaluated by a qualified professional counselor. These behaviors can, at times, be symptoms of other disruptions in the child's life, such as being bullied, suffering significant grief or loss, or the birth or arrival of a new family member.

Teaching a child from a young age, through words and actions, that every human being's life and safety is precious and is to be guarded promotes a culture of nonviolence. This is the greatest violence prevention "program" we can give to our children. When we demonstrate through our actions that we will not tolerate violence in our personal lives, our children have an opportunity to internalize nonviolence as a life value. Children can learn to get their needs met without the use of violent behavior.

Unfortunately, negative societal influences can impact children in negative ways, whether through media, entertainment, or other family members. The creative challenge is to create a protected safe home base while supporting healthy social interaction for our children. This includes raising them with the understanding that the police will be called if a person is harmed by their violent behavior. Raising your children to be responsible and accountable for their own actions is a powerful and preventative message for them.

Talking Down Someone Who Is Making Violent Threats

It is beyond the scope of this book regarding extended detail for crisis intervention related to violent behavior. When a person in the irrational zone crosses the line by making threats—either by words, behavior, or bodily harm—and you feel your life is genuinely in jeopardy, call 9-1-1. Still, there are script options for diffusing a child or adolescent whose behavior is escalating to the point of being threatening behavior.

In the event you feel that your personal well-being is in jeopardy, call the person by his first name and give clear direction in a strong, firm voice. Be aware of your own anxiety level, and stay in control of your emotions without panicking.

"I need you to slow down because the words you are using right now sound like a threat. Get yourself under control and stop the threatening words, or I will call 9-1-1."

"Put down the [object] and calm down, or I will call 9-1-1 to get help from the police."

If a child or adolescent has threatened violence with an object or weapon, I recommend that a qualified mental health professional evaluate him. Contacting your child's primary care professional is also important, as there may be a need to screen for factors such as mood-altering substances or a medical condition that could be causing the escalated aggressive behavior.

This chapter has covered some emotionally intense subject matter, to be sure. Familiarizing yourself with these concepts and skills will help equip you in your task of parenting, even if you never need to use them all. It is a little like learning self-defense techniques. Learning them will give you confidence to handle a variety of situations—and hopefully, you won't need to put them to use. As you have a clearer awareness of your own emotions and personal boundaries, your wisdom will increase, and your confidence in your parental role will grow.

PART 5

Putting It All Together

CHAPTER 10

Parent Job Description and Evaluating Parental Performance

This chapter will review the specific responsibilities of parenting and consider strategies for increasing effectiveness and consistency, while supporting self-compassion and self-esteem for any past mistakes or regrets. We will start with a brief review of basic parenting principles.

Positive Parenting Principles
- Give a gift to your children by making your health and wellness a priority, including being addiction-free. You'll have more energy to care for your kids.
- Establish age-appropriate and consistent house rules and boundaries.
- Remember that what you do carries more weight and influence in your children's lives than what you say.
- Practice being slow to anger (James 1:19), which not only is effective but allows a window of time to think about an appropriate response and reduces the likelihood of an unwanted overreaction.
- Huddle, communicate, and develop a unified response or plan with your spouse.

- Be consistent.
- Be open to modifying the plan after mutual discussion (separate from the child). It is okay to change your mind. Ensure the change is logical and you both agree to it.
- Back each other up, maintaining a unified front between primary parent figures in the home.

The Parenting Job Description

With this review of some of the fundamentals of child development, it's now time to look more closely at the parent's job. Yes, *job*. While it is true that healthy parenting is grounded in a relationship of care and commitment, it is also very helpful to identify the various tasks and functions that, together, form effective nurture and care for a child. The following section on Evaluating Parental Role Performance will show how constructive it can be to separate the person from the behavior. This allows parents to evaluate the positives and negatives of their parenting without diminishing their value as a person.

People benefit from a description of the duties and responsibilities of a position, role, or job. A job description gives a person a clearer understanding of the expectations and actions needed to perform that role or job effectively. I suggest the following list of key elements for a parent job description gleaned from experience working with children and families, with examples of tasks that support each category. These are not intended to be complete or exhaustive lists. Additional suggestions are included in the corresponding items at the end of this chapter.

Provide Basic Needs
- Food
- Clean drinking water
- Clothing
- Adequate shelter

Provide Safety and Security

- Prevent neglect—children are not responsible for taking on work, household tasks, or preparing meals at too early an age
- Teach personal safety rules
- Prevent victimization with age-appropriate education of refusal skills and being aware of one's surroundings

Ensure Medical and Health Needs

- Physical—nurture the child when treating "owies"
- Emotional—show empathy and compassion

Teach Right from Wrong, Including by Example

- Teach respect for others—including others' property—and that people are more important than things
- Attend to spiritual care
- Teach positive identity
- Model positive values and ethics you desire your child to learn
- Avoid double-standard ("Do as I say, not as I do")

Care for and Nurture the Child

- Healthy hugs and kisses
- Comfort
- Encouragement
- Healthy touch

Teach Discipline with Reasonable Limits

- Use good judgment; don't discipline out of anger or rage

Teach Personal Grooming and Hygiene

- Dental hygiene
- Physical hygiene (encourage bathing/showering; use of deodorant after onset of puberty)
- Sex education (provide age-appropriate sexual development information)

Teach and Model Problem-Solving Skills
- Prevent drug/alcohol abuse (see the list of problem-solving steps under the correlating item at the end of this chapter)

Coordinate Educational Needs
- Communicate with educators to whom you have delegated parts of your child's education

Teach Social Skills
- Model taking turns, use of manners, etc.

Teach and Model Assertive Communication Skills
- Encourage language development and reading skills (example: nighttime reading time with your child)

Provide and Coordinate Recreational Needs
- Age-appropriate exercise
- Opportunities for athletics/team sports

Provide 24-Hour Care
- Coordinate check-ins with trusted and responsible adults after school hours
- Ensure supervision/accountability until the child is eighteen or legally emancipated

Teach Age-Appropriate Independent Living Skills
- Household chores
- Laundry
- Managing finances
- Learning to drive

I am a human being. You are a human being. And as human beings, we are imperfect. We make mistakes. We are not all-powerful, nor are we all-knowing. There are no perfect parents, as there are no perfect people on the planet. As imperfect parents, we have limitations.

For example, we cannot be in multiple places simultaneously—we cannot be physically and mentally at our place of employment and simultaneously be personally nurturing and protecting our children. We may be limited in our parental role because of various external factors like:

- Work schedules
- Health concerns on the part of the parent/s; health concerns on the part of the child
- Financial concerns/limitations
- A neighborhood's crime rate
- The level of alcohol or drug abuse in a neighborhood, school, or home

"Good enough" parenting is an attainable goal. "Good enough" parenting doesn't mean settling for an inadequate minimum standard of parenting but that parents have options to adequately provide for their children's needs within their human limitations. Parents don't need to be paralyzed by fears magnified by the unrealistic expectations of perfectionism. Healthy parents learn to compensate for limitations.

Compensating for our limitations can involve various adaptive and creative strategies. For example, to compensate for the inability to perform one of the essential responsibilities of the parenting job description, a parent might delegate specific parenting tasks to trustworthy support people. Healthy compensating for limitations frequently involves expanding a support system.

Evaluating Parental Role Performance

The practice of evaluating one's performance has been around for a long time. Reviews by professional music critics and juried music competitions are examples of music performance evaluations. In American culture, such performance acknowledgments and awards include Teacher of the Year, Student of the Quarter, and Salesperson of the Year. In some industries, yearly employee performance reviews are mandatory.

Let's study a typical employee review to establish helpful parallels in evaluating the parent's performance. The yearly review typically has two components. First, the employee completes a self-evaluation of their strengths and weaknesses regarding the job performance. Second, the employer or a designated representative provides the employee with constructive feedback regarding the quality and competency of behavior and skill in performing the responsibilities of the job. A performance review can improve the employee's confidence and effectiveness. When the employee has difficulty adequately performing their duties, it is appropriate to receive additional training to obtain or strengthen their knowledge and skills. Once sufficiently trained, they are then responsible for performing the job consistently. Were the employee to violate the established ethical code of conduct or the expectations of the job description, disciplinary measures, along with corrective steps, would be implemented. Depending on the severity of infractions or the number and frequency of repeated violations, the employee may be at risk of discipline. Progressive corrective steps could include a verbal warning, a written warning, suspension, a fine (as in professional sports), administrative leave, or termination from the position (particularly in ethical conduct violations in which the rights/safety of others have been violated).

Similarly, parents can enhance their confidence and effectiveness by evaluating strengths and weaknesses related to their parenting role. "Good enough" parenting occurs when the care and parenting are done "well enough" to promote a child's healthy development. Again, there is no perfect human being on the planet, so there are no perfect parents.

I invite you to be open and honest as you review this section of self-evaluation. But please avoid the following two extreme reactions to this material:

- Taking on false guilt out of tendencies for perfectionism
- Becoming defensive and closed off to a fresh perspective on one of the oldest roles/jobs in human history: parenting

This section is not intended to evaluate other people. Concern yourself with evaluating only your parenting job. The foundation of being able to objectively evaluate a parent's role and performance is illustrated in the following Diagram A:

Value as a human being	How well I perform my role
Identity	How healthy I am
Who I am: created in the image of God with the capacity for a relationship with my Creator	Quality of relationships
	Quality of life: good, fair, poor
	Standard of living
	Limitations: physical, emotional, financial
	Need to focus on positive strengths
	Compensate for my limitations with strengths
	Deposits (+) when things are going well
	Withdrawals (−) challenges or losses

It is easier and less threatening to evaluate our performance when we are more secure in our personal value. However, many people tend to be brutally unforgiving of their mistakes but would be understanding and merciful toward someone else who made the same ones. Just as we've learned not to shame our children for making a mistake but to help them learn from it, parents need not beat themselves up for their mistakes but learn and grow from them. We need to identify areas needing improvement and be open to fresh options to be more effective in our parenting.

For those who are not yet parents, use this section as positive preparation to avoid the landmines and mistakes generations of parents have made.

Diagram A represents the two "bank accounts" that contribute to a person's self-concept: how we think and feel about ourselves. The bank account on the left reflects the intrinsic value of a human being—represented by the icon of the gold bars that never deplete or erode. The value of a person is grounded in their identity as a member of the human race. Human inalienable rights flow from the reality of intrinsic human value and are universal, transcending cultural traditions, politics, religious beliefs, and socioeconomic status. This is the basis for humanitarian relief efforts when a large-scale natural disaster hits any part of the world. Being created in the image of God as a human being includes the capacity to be in relationship with our Creator. All human beings possess *intrinsic value*, regardless of their world and life view, belief system, or cognitive/physical health/functioning level.

The bank account on the right represents a more fluid component of self-concept. This is the feedback we receive from ourselves and others on how well *we do* in our roles. This bank account has deposits and withdrawals. Challenges to our physical or mental health, like losses—a job, home, significant relationship—are examples of limitations of and withdrawals from this account.

We increase our quality of life when we live in balance, acknowledge and live within our human limitations, and compensate for those limitations/deficits/disabilities/challenges by focusing on our strengths. Putting our identity as a valued human being as the foundation of our core value frees us to deal with the ups and downs of life without going existentially bankrupt. We can better endure seasons of poor health, unemployment, financial hardship, and other losses. I am intentionally not using the commonly used terms self-esteem and self-worth. Over the years, these terms can be interpreted to mean different things. So for this discussion, I am operationally defining the elements of self-concept using the two bank accounts illustrated in Diagram A.

Separating the person from his behavior is grace-based. Just because a person made a mistake does not make him a mistake. Mistakes can be forgiven, and some require restitution, particularly when they affect the lives and rights of other people.

The following list of parenting tasks and the accompanying diagram incorporate the specific parental responsibilities as described earlier in this chapter. The bank account on the right side of the Diagram B contains a graph, which you can use to self-evaluate present or past parenting. Whether you are a new parent, a longtime parent, or a future parent, use this diagram and the information in this chapter to reflect on the quality of your parenting job.

Evaluate your parenting in response to each question and according to each of your children. Rate your effectiveness as well as your effort. Use the following guide to help you in your evaluation.

1. Have I consistently provided for the safety and security needs of this child?

You cannot protect your child 100 percent of the time—you'd need a personal SWAT team or bodyguard to escort your child wherever she goes. Life is unfair, and sometimes things happen over which you have no control and for which you are not responsible.

2. Have I consistently established healthy boundaries to promote protection for my child from the effects of drugs and alcohol?

If your alcohol use or other mood-altering substances prevents you from fully functioning as the protective and emotionally engaged parent you want to be, I urge you to reach out for assistance. Locate a qualified and compassionate professional licensed to provide a substance use disorder evaluation, assess the need for a medically supported (managed or monitored) detox, and help you develop a relapse prevention plan. Remember that withdrawal from alcohol that is not medically supported can be life-threatening.

3. Have I consistently been involved in my child's schooling and education?

This could include being intentional about your child's school placement and being involved in parent-teacher conferences. Your child's education includes teaching your child by example—modeling desired behaviors. It can also include establishing fun activities with your child, such as:

- Reading with your child (perhaps before your child's bedtime) and having your child read a favorite story to you, allowing him to show what he can do. Regularly check out children's books from your local library. Make reading a fun habit.
- Taking your child on trips to such things as the zoo, an aquarium, a museum, a musical performance, a play, etc.

4. Have I consistently taught personal hygiene and modeled it by example?

This includes ensuring children are appropriately bathing when young to establish good hygiene habits that will continue into adulthood and educating them on the necessity of showers and deodorant as they reach puberty and adolescence.

5. Have I provided age-appropriate information regarding human sexual development?

This is a broad subject that includes related topics:

- Age-appropriate truthful information regarding where babies come from
- Education about private parts, privacy boundaries, and "good touch" (to prevent sexual victimization)
- Discussion about anticipated body changes in adolescence before the emergence of secondary sex characteristics (such as a daughter's first menstrual period or a son's voice change and growth of body hair)

6. Did I take good care of myself while pregnant? (For mothers)

7. Have I addressed my own health needs, including any addiction recovery?

8. Have I prioritized meeting my child's medical needs from infancy through the teen years?

Medical care includes physical health, mental health, and substance abuse recovery. Have you emotionally and financially supported your child's medical care, including providing transportation to appointments?

9. Have I taught my child the difference between right and wrong?

10. Have I prioritized legal and ethical behavior as an example to my child?

11. Have I asked for forgiveness regarding mistakes?

Have you taught your child about "grace" (unearned favor), unconditional love, and acceptance? Even better, do you model it?

12. Do I have a fair and consistent system of setting boundaries and administering discipline for my child from age two to seventeen?

Refer to chapter 8 regarding age-appropriate discipline, and don't forget about giving your child opportunities to learn about "natural consequences."

13. Am I teaching my child age-appropriate social skills?

- Manners, such as saying, "Please" and "Thank you"
- Waiting to take turns when playing with others (such as when playing board games)

- Skills for making friends, like sharing toys, playing well with others, listening, sharing feelings and opinions, remembering that an opinion is not a fact, and not allowing bullying behavior

14. Do I promote and incorporate recreation into my child's life?
- Taking her for walks on a safe route
- Playing with him on his level (indoor/outdoor games)
- Involvement with organized team sports
- Involvement in school-sponsored activities
- Involvement in community organizations, such as scouting and 4-H

15. Do I model, teach, and promote assertive communication?
- You tell the truth
- You are polite and respectful of other people
- You ask for what you need
- You say what you mean and mean what you say
- You use listening skills
- You read to your child
- You have your child read to you at an age-appropriate level
- You have taught your child your first language

16. Do I model and teach healthy problem-solving and decision-making?
- You avoid impulsive, reactionary decisions
- You avoid impulsive buying that results in taking money from other basic necessities (such as budgeted funds for shelter, food, transportation, health care, etc.)
- You guard against substance abuse and strive for addiction prevention
- You practice the practical problem-solving model:
  ✓ Identify the problem
  ✓ Gather direct information regarding the problem, needs, and concerns

✓ Identify options for solutions
✓ Brainstorm pros and cons (positives and negatives) for each option, including an estimate of possible consequences
✓ Identify any time pressures
✓ Make a decision
✓ Evaluate outcome and make any needed adjustments

17. Do I consistently care for and nurture my child?

- You demonstrate comfort
- You use encouraging words and actions
- You give healthy hugs and kisses, with appropriate boundaries

18. Do I coordinate and delegate appropriate supervision from birth to legal emancipation, including ensuring school attendance?

- You are legally responsible for the actions of your children until they are eighteen years old or legally emancipated

Diagram B for parenting self-evaluation:

Value as a human being

Identity: who I am

Created in the image of God with the capacity for a relationship with my Creator

How well I perform my parental responsibilities

	Great	Good	Poor	Needs Support	Needs Intervention
1. Provide basic needs					
2. Provide safety and security					
3. Protect from drugs and alcohol					
4. Ensure schooling and education					
5. Teach hygiene and information on sexual development					
6. Followed prenatal care guidelines					
7. Address my own health needs					
8. Address my child's health needs					
9. Teach right and wrong					
10. Make legal and ethical choices					
11. Ask for forgiveness for mistakes when appropriate					
12. Discipline fairly and set limits					
13. Teach social skills					
14. Encourage recreation and fun					
15. Teach respectful communication					
16. Teach problem-solving skills					
17. Care for and nurture my child					
18. Supervise adequately					

By being honest with yourself in rating your effectiveness in the parenting job description, you have done a courageous thing. I encourage you to review your areas of strength and celebrate them. Take a moment to reflect on the positive influences in your life that have contributed to your parenting strengths. Be grateful for them.

Now take a moment and identify any items that can benefit from improvement. Remember, there are no perfect parents. For example, many fathers can have a measure of denial about the seriousness of a child's injury or illness, minimizing the need to take the time and resources to have the child checked out by a physician delaying such access. This can be particularly true for parents who personally have a high pain threshold or who have not gone to healthcare professionals much themselves.

Much of human behavior is learned. After reading this book, if you become aware of problems that prevent you from being emotionally present to adequately provide for the needs of your child, I strongly urge you to reach out for support. Professional counseling with a qualified and compassionate provider can bring good results. Parenting classes are available in many communities. Contact your local hospital or go online for a list of resources in your area. Help is available, but it is your responsibility to search for it until you find it.

In my work at The Center • A Place of HOPE, I frequently hear of people's lengthy quest for treatment resources and the relief they experience when they find the support that fits their needs. The structured treatment program at The Center may be the supportive, multidisciplinary team environment you need to help you address and heal from the impact of landmines in your life. Don't give up. Persist in your search for the resources and support you need. (See the list of resources at the back of this book.)

PART 6

Stories of Heartbreak and Inspiration

CHAPTER **11**

Two Real-Life Stories

We live in a broken world. It is a mixture of beauty and danger, joy and pain. And we never know which variety of "flavor" is coming our way next. As finite humans, we cannot see the future or anticipate unexpected changes to our plans. As shown, a parent's hopes and dreams for the nurture and raising of their child are sometimes radically altered.

I conclude this book by sharing two real-life stories that involve pain and love, trauma and hope. May these stories encourage and inspire you as you write your parenting story.

Karen's Story

Karen isn't her real name. She permitted me to share the basics of her story to encourage others provided names would be changed to protect confidentiality.

Many years ago, Karen contacted The Center for outpatient counseling services for help with personal insecurities and relationship problems. Karen had fallen for a guy who appeared to be incapable of committing to her completely—or not willing. She found herself caught in an internal tug of war. On the one hand, she valued marriage as the context for love and a lifelong commitment. On the other hand, she feared losing a relationship with a man to whom she had attached her heart. Incredible stress, insecurity, and anxiety resulted as she attempted to set boundaries in the relationship to live more consistently with her internal values and integrity.

Then we reviewed her history. It turns out this was not the first time she had attached her heart to someone unwilling or unable to commit to her. When Karen was a high school student, she became pregnant. This unplanned pregnancy quickly became a crisis pregnancy. Because of an unfortunate stigma of shame, her family required her to move out of her home when she started to show signs of being pregnant. Karen was sent away to live with an extended family member who lived a long distance from her home. Karen went through her pregnancy without the support of her family and friends, displaced from her home, community, and education,

Karen's focus turned inward to the little life she carried. She quickly bonded with that little one. (Look again at the photo at the beginning of part 2 for a visual reminder of what a four-and-a-half-month-old baby in the womb looks like.) Karen sang to her baby and talked to her. Yes, an ultrasound confirmed she was carrying a little girl—her daughter.

She looked forward to her daughter's birth with great anticipation. She decided to keep and raise her baby, naming her Katie.

As the pregnancy progressed, relationship stressors escalated. The baby's father was not willing to be involved or committed. Karen found herself facing difficult choices. Because of a turn of traumatic circumstances, she experienced unyielding pressure to place Katie up for adoption. Karen experienced the trauma of not keeping and parenting her daughter as she had dreamed and planned.

At that time, closed adoption was the only option available to her. So Karen's traumatic loss was further compounded by the terms of the closed adoption. Not only would she not be legally permitted to have contact with her daughter after surrendering her parental rights, but she would not know with whom her daughter would be placed. The adoption file was sealed. Karen would not be able to search for her daughter until her daughter reached the age of eighteen. She was devastated and heartbroken.

Today, most adoptions can be "open," in which the child's birth parents can select not only who will receive the high privilege of raising the child but also the faith orientation of the adoptive parents. Open adoption provides a structure for an exchange of contact information, updated pictures of the child, and customized arrangements for visitation. (See your local adoption agency for further information regarding open adoption.)

Karen would always be Katie's birth mother, but losing custody of Katie was a traumatic landmine. To survive emotionally, Karen needed to shift her focus elsewhere. Karen was a woman of faith and continued to pray to God for her daughter's protection and care throughout her growing-up years, even without the benefit of seeing her daughter develop from an infant to the young woman she would meet many years later.

Karen contacted one of several agencies that legally conduct searches for now-adult children who had been placed in closed adoptions. A few years before she reached out to The Center for counseling support, she providentially was able to identify and locate her daughter, who had been renamed: Angela. Karen made the courageous decision to reach out and make contact, not knowing how her daughter would respond. Karen wanted to make sure Angela knew how much she had been wanted and loved and see if some kind of relationship was possible now that she and Angela were adults.

Angela had been adopted by loving and nurturing parents who provided well for her. At the time Karen gave permission to include her story in this book, she was working hard to cultivate an evolving relationship and friendship with Angela and her adoptive family. She described it as a work in progress.

God had answered her prayers, and Karen was grateful. She began trusting God with her future. As she processed the past traumatic loss, she gradually grew more confident in herself and set better, healthy boundaries.

It is worth reflecting on the developmental landmines (presented in part 3) that impacted Karen as an adolescent, which resulted in certain behaviors as an adult. She and her high school boyfriend set themselves up for a crisis pregnancy by not waiting until they wanted or were able to commit to a healthy long-term relationship with each another and not practicing birth control as part of their choice to become sexually active. Recall that society, including families, need to support the formation of the older adolescent's positive core identity and sense of purpose. The individual at this life stage has a God-designed need to be treated fairly and included in the decision-making process regarding their own lives. According to Karen's report, her family allowed shame and their need to maintain a positive image and reputation in the community to highjack Karen's decision-making and undermined her legitimate need to be involved in that process regarding her baby girl. All indications are that Karen's parents treated her as a child and coerced her to give up the daughter she had become strongly attached to during her pregnancy.

Any older adolescent in Karen's position would be at significant risk of increased hopelessness and possibly suicidal thoughts and behaviors—particularly after being forced to give up a loved child in a closed adoption, never knowing if they would see their precious child again. It's a reflection of God's providential grace in Karen's life that she did not become despondent to the point of taking her life after the crushing loss of her daughter. By God's grace, Karen also retained her Christian faith without pushing God away and continued to pray for her daughter in the years that followed. Karen demonstrated psychological, emotional, and spiritual strength and resilience during extreme stress points in her life.

Prayer was a key factor in her locating her daughter through an extensive search process. Prayer paved the way for her courageous decision to reach out and contact her adult daughter. Karen's example of calling out to her Lord in her distress and embracing her life is encouraging and inspiring. She found purpose in her undying love and intercessory prayer for her daughter's well-being. I can only imagine that Karen's prayers for her daughter continue to be lifted up as a sweet fragrance to the One who hears. Jeremiah 29:12–14a (NIV) states:

"'Then you will call on me and come and pray to me, and I will listen to you. You will seek me and find me when you seek me with all your heart. I will be found by you,' declares the LORD."

Karen's story is an inspiring example of a mother's enduring prayers for her lost child. She describes her belief that the Lord heard her heartfelt pleas and responded by facilitating the sweet reunion with Angela. Karen's prayers for her precious one continue. It is a powerful reminder to pray for our children and to invite others to regularly lift us up in prayer to support us in our role as parents.

Regrettably, many women throughout history have a similar story to Karen's. Hopefully, with the shift from closed adoptions to open adoptions, some aspects of Karen's heartbreak will not be experienced by people in similar situations in the future.

The next story comes from American history and highlights the role of a grandmother to support and fireproof her young granddaughter amid battle.

Tessie's Story: A Grandmother's Gift of Endurance

Robert Coles documented an inspirational and historical story from the early days of desegregation. The setting was New Orleans, Louisiana, 1961. Six-year-old Tessie was one of four African American schoolgirls on the front line of school desegregation in New Orleans.

Every day for several months, angry adults verbally assaulted Tessie and her three young classmates with strings of racial slurs and obscenities as federal marshals escorted the girls to school through the mob of protesters. In efforts to scare, intimidate, and prevent Tessie and her friends from attending the previously all-white McDonough Elementary School, protesters also hurled violent death threats at the little girls.

After several months of this traumatic onslaught, the strain of the mob's hatred finally wore Tessie down. She begged her parents not to go back to that school with all the angry people. Tessie's grandmother lovingly and compassionately came to her granddaughter's side. I imagine she wrapped Tessie in a hug as she told Tessie how sorry she was that she could not go with her to the school and "call these people to my side, and read to them from the Bible, and tell them, remind them, that He's up there, Jesus, watching over all of us—it don't matter who you are and what your skin color is."[53]

Coles' account tells of the grandmother stopping to swat at a bee that had made its way into the kitchen. She picked it up, and after seeing that it was still alive, that she'd only stunned it, she took it outside and set it free. She then returned to Tessie with this profoundly wise life lesson:

> You see, my child, you have to help the good Lord with his world! He puts us here, and he calls us to help him out. That bee doesn't belong here, it belongs out there. You belong in that McDonough School, and there will be a day when everyone knows that, even those poor folks—Lord, I pray for them! Those poor, poor folks who are out there shouting their heads off at you. You're one of the Lord's people; he's put his hand on you. He's given a call to you, a call to service—in his name! There's all those people, scared out of their minds, and by the time you're ready to leave the McDonough School, they'll be calmed down, and they won't be paying you no mind at all, child, and I'll guarantee you, that's how it will be![54]

Tessie's grandmother went on to tell her: "We're the lucky ones to be called, and we've got to prove we can do what the Lord wants, that we're up to it."

By living and teaching her faith, Tessie's grandmother gave Tessie the amazing gift of being able to embrace an honorable purpose and have compassion for her oppressors ("those poor, poor folks"). But she also insulated Tessie, to some degree, from the otherwise traumatizing effects of the violent racism in her community. She lovingly and powerfully helped Tessie navigate a minefield of racial hatred.

As we reflect on the developmental landmines that impacted Karen in the previous story, so, too, can we benefit from applying our understanding of developmental needs and risks to Tessie in this story. The developmental tasks of early school age (5–7 years) are sex-role identification, early moral development, concrete cognitive operations, and group play. The psychosocial crisis is "Initiative [child's exploration of her world] versus Guilt."

Regarding Tessie, we first consider the destructive impact of the angry mob. Normal, healthy six-year-olds look for adult role models who accept them and whom they can follow. From these models, the children begin to internalize values and develop a sense of right and wrong from role models. Tessie and her classmates were exposed to the mob's verbal and emotional violence, which is a form of warfare.

Psychological warfare has been an effective instrument that hostile countries have used against adults for centuries. If it can traumatize and debilitate adults, how much more does this type of violence inflict lasting harm on vulnerable children? The federal marshals' presence apparently prevented the children from being physically assaulted, dragged away, or worse. Physical assault, however, is not required to inflict lasting harm on the victim. The verbal threats, condemnation, and rejection targeted these young children where they were most vulnerable. Tessie and her peers of color were at risk of internalizing the mob's venom after months of daily bombardment that said they were bad, deserved being screamed at, and were doing something terribly wrong by walking into that school.

The children would also have been vulnerable to confusion, perhaps wondering, "How is it that white folks who say they are Christians are not showing love and compassion to me?" Some of those children were themselves at risk of becoming hateful and rejecting the Christian faith because many—if not most—of the angry people claimed to follow that religion. They were at risk of coming away from their experience with the perception and belief that all white people hated them. Healing requires the truth to be repeatedly spoken louder than the distorted lies. Tessie and her peers were at risk of retreating and hiding in the safety of their homes instead of exploring their world. The traumatic effects of the mob's racial violence put these young children at risk of severe anxiety, nightmares, and disrupted emotional development.

From a developmental perspective, Tessie's grandmother gave her healing gifts, including the gift of seeing what stick-to-it-iveness looks like—not giving up in the face of adversity. Another healing gift was the introduction to post-conventional thought in Stage 4 of moral development: being willing to forgive those who persecute you, show compassion toward your persecutors, and endure for the greater good. Wow! This was needed, especially because the political and legal authorities did not have the support or the will to arrest and prosecute protesters who were committing verbal assault and making death threats against the girls. Tessie's grandmother's love and compassion were like a healing balm to help Tessie to begin to mend the injury from the landmines of the mob's verbal violence. These gifts also served to help immunize Tessie against hatred.

We could certainly use more of that today. We could benefit from taking a page from the grandmother's forgiveness playbook. Tessie's grandmother presented herself as that strong female role model that, developmentally, Tessie was primed to follow. Remember, early school-age children operate from conventional thought, in which the opinions and beliefs of an important authority figure set the moral compass they value and eventually internalize. "If my grandmother said it, it must be true."

The fact that Cole's book was published tells us that McDonough Elementary School was eventually successfully desegregated. This means that Tessie's grandmother's prophetic words came to pass: "... and by the time you're ready to leave the McDonough School, they'll be calmed down, and they won't be paying you no mind at all, child, and I guarantee you, that's how it will be!"

Besides being the voice of truth in Tessie's life, this grandmother gave her granddaughter the vision that the horrifying trial she was experiencing was *temporary*—short-term; not lasting forever. And that message carries the gift of hope. Grandparents and other extended family members have an amazing opportunity to speak and pray positive vision, hope, and wisdom into a child's life. Tessie's grandmother likely spoke from personal experience of enduring great hardship and adversity. She was Tessie's hero that day of trial and during the days to follow. I honor Tessie's grandmother, as well as Tessie, by including their story here.

I trust these stories have inspired you and planted hope in your heart despite any heartbreak you may have experienced.

In Closing

Thank you for joining me on this journey. I trust you have gained a greater understanding of your child's developmental needs. These keys will empower you to live your life with more confidence as you parent your children more effectively. May you and your children thrive as you continue into the next chapter of life's journey.

I'd love to hear from you, whether you have a success story to share or need further support through the whole-person care program at The Center • A Place of HOPE. The toll-free number is 1-877-771-5166. You may also contact us online at www.aplaceofhope.com.

I close with this prayer of blessing, which I have respectfully adapted from the public domain words of the ancient Celtic prayer known as an Irish Blessing:

> May the road rise up to meet you and your family
>   in the journey of life.
> May the wind be always at your back.
> May the sun shine warm upon your face; the rains
>   fall soft upon your fields.
> May you find shelter when the storms of life rage
>   around you.
> And until we meet again, may God hold you and
>   your precious ones in the palm of his hand.

Let it be so.

Resources

Rich Bimler, *Sex and the New You, Book 4* (for ages 11–14) in the Learning about Sex series, (Concordia Publishing House), 2015.

Foster Cline and Jim Fay, *Parenting with Love and Logic*, Updated and Expanded Edition, (Tyndale House), 2006.

Dr. Gregory Jantz, PhD, and Michael Gurian, LMFT, with Ann McMurray, *Raising Boys by Design: What the Bible and Brain Science Reveal about What Boys Need to Thrive* (WaterBrook Press), 2013.

Dr. Gregory Jantz, PhD, and Dr. Tim Clinton, EdD, with Ann McMurray, *Don't Call It Love: Breaking the Cycle of Relationship Dependency* (Revell), 2015.

Dr. Gregory Jantz, PhD, with Ann McMurray, *Healing the Scars of Emotional Abuse*, Revised and Updated (Revell), 2009.

Cynthia Ulrich Tobias, *You Can't Make Me (But I Can Be Persuaded)* Revised and Updated Edition (WaterBrook Press), 1999.

For more information on The Center • A Place of HOPE, call the toll-free number: 1-888-771-5166, or visit us online at www.aplaceofhope.com.

About the Author

Mike Weiford is a clinical social worker and child mental health specialist with a total of forty-one years of experience in behavioral health. For the last thirty-two years, he has been a trusted therapist on the staff of The Center • A Place of Hope, located in Edmonds, Washington.

Mike has a Master of Social Work and is licensed as an independent clinical social worker. He draws wisdom from his many years of counseling children, adolescents, families, couples, and individual adults. Mike integrates his experience of supporting and empowering parents into *Navigating the Minefield*.

Mike is currently employed as part of The Center's multidisciplinary partial hospitalization care team. He has been married for thirty-nine years to his wife, Judy. They are the parents of three grown children and two grandchildren. They make their home in Mountlake Terrace, Washington.

Notes

Introduction

1   Rick Gladstone, "Land Mine Casualties Jump 75% as Funding for Their Removal Declines," *New York Times*, November 22, 2016, https://www.nytimes.com/2016/11/22/world/land-mine-casualties-annual-report.html.

Chapter 1

2   Lennart Nilsson and Lars Hamberger, MD, *A Child Is Born* (New York: Dell, 1986), 124.

3   Nilsson and Hamberger, 124.

4   Barbara and Philip Newman, *Development Through Life: A Psychosocial Approach*, Revised Edition (Illinois: The Dorsey Press 1979), 49–52.

5   Gregory L Jantz, PhD and Michael Gurian with Ann McMurray, *Raising Boys by Design: What the Bible and Brain Science Reveal about What Boys Need to Thrive* (WaterBrook Press 2013), 19–21, 23, 26. I recommend reviewing this book for a more in-depth discussion of findings from research involving brain scan imaging: PET, fMRI, and SPECT scans of male and female brains.

6   Jantz and Gurian, *Raising Boys*, 31.

7   Jantz and Gurian, *Raising Boys*, 31.

Chapter 2

8   Jantz and Gurian, *Raising Boys*, 186.

9   Jantz and Gurian, *Raising Boys*, 87.

10 Jantz and Gurian, *Raising Boys*, 96.

11 Jantz and Gurian, *Raising Boys*, 12.

12 Jantz and Gurian, *Raising Boys*, 92.

13 Jantz and Gurian, *Raising Boys*, 93.

14 Jantz and Gurian, *Raising Boys*, 94.

15 Jantz and Gurian, *Raising Boys*, 86–87.

16 Jantz and Gurian, *Raising Boys*, 87.

17 Jantz and Gurian, *Raising Boys*, 110–11.

18 Jantz and Gurian, *Raising Boys*, 111.

19 Anthony Norcia and Faraz Farzin of Stanford Vision and Neurodevelopment Lab, "Infant Facial Recognition," *Stanford Report*, December 11, 2012.

20 Norcia and Farzin, "Infant."

21 Newman, *Development Through Life, 13th Edition* (Cengage Learning; 2017), 110.

22 Newman, *Development*, 110.

23 Newman, *Development*, 110.

Chapter 3

24 Newman, *Development Through Life, 13th Edition* (Cengage Learning; 2017), 134.

25 Newman, *Development*, 122–23.

26 Newman, *Development*, 128.

27 Newman, *Development*, 144.

28 Newman, *Development*, 129.

29 Newman, *Development*, 131.

30 Newman, *Development*, 133.

31 Newman, *Development*, 140.

32 Newman, *Development*, 140.

Chapter 4

33 Newman, *Development Through Life, 13th Edition* (Cengage Learning; 2017), 191.

34 Newman, *Development*, 177.

35 Newman, *Development*, 177–78.

36 Michael Gurian, *The Minds of Girls: A New Path for Raising Healthy, Resilient, and Successful Women* (Gurian Institute Press, 2018), 16–17.

37 Gurian, *Minds*, 180.

38 Gurian, *Minds*, 186.

39 Gurian, *Minds*, 190.

40 Gurian, *Minds*, 194.

Chapter 5
41 Newman, *Development Through Life, 13th Edition* (Cengage Learning; 2017), 229.

42 Newman, *Development Through Life*, 233.

43 Newman, *Development Through Life*, 238.

44 Newman, *Development Through Life*, 235.

Chapter 6
45 Newman, *Development Through Life, 13th Edition* (Cengage Learning; 2017), 229.

46 Newman, *Development Through Life*, 233.

47 Newman, *Development Through Life*, 238.

48 Newman, *Development Through Life*, 235.

Chapter 8
49 Newman, *Development Through Life, 13th Edition* (Cengage Learning; 2017), 151.

50 Newman, *Development Through Life*, 164.

51 Newman, *Development Through Life*, 151.

52 Newman, *Development Through Life*, 151–52.

Chapter 11
53 Robert Coles, *The Call of Service: A Witness to Idealism* (Boston/New York: Houghton Mifflin, 1993), 3–4.

54 Robert Coles, *The Call of Service*, 3-4.

ORDER INFORMATION

To order additional copies of this book, please visit
www.redemption-press.com.
Also available on Amazon.com and BarnesandNoble.com
or by calling toll-free 1-844-2REDEEM.

CPSIA information can be obtained
at www.ICGtesting.com
Printed in the USA
BVHW010559150322
631321BV00003B/12

9 781646 454556